The

BOMB VESSEL

GRANADO

1742

**Anatomy
of the
Ship**

The

BOMB VESSEL

GRANADO

1742

Peter Goodwin

Naval
Institute
Press

Frontispiece

1. The bomb vessel *Granado* of 1742: a port bow view of the fine model by Bob Lightley in the National Maritime Museum, Greenwich. *National Maritime Museum*

Published and distributed in the United States of America and Canada by the Naval Institute Press Annapolis, Maryland 21402

Library of Congress Catalog Card No 89-62379

ISBN 0–87021–178–1

Manufactured in Great Britain

Contents

Foreword

The development and history of the bomb vessel have often been masked by the more major events of naval history. With the exception of the works of a few writers, little has been written on this subject. Yet the initial conception of this form of ship both revolutionised naval assault tactics and generated considerable improvements in artillery, paving the way to the introduction of the rifled shell-firing gun during the nineteenth century.

For various reasons, I have based this work on Bob Lightley's superb detailed model of the *Granado* (1742), now on permanent display at the National Maritime Museum at Greenwich. Although this particular ship does not represent the generally accepted bomb vessel design, its individuality has proved an intriguing subject. Apart from the unusual aspects of its construction, this ship presents a combination of interesting features, including the sea mortars, conventional carriage guns and swivel guns. With regard to sailing performance, she was ketch-rigged, but on occasion could also be propelled by oars. Internally, she had an unconventional layout, centred around two heavily built shell rooms.

Naturally, I would not have been able to produce this work without the assistance of various colleagues and institutions, for source material, plans and photographic services. I must therefore express my thanks to the staff of the Draught Room at the National Maritime Museum, for providing the various necessary plans. Second, I wish to thank the following National Maritime Museum members of staff for their individual services: Fred Walker, David Lyon and Dr Eric Kently; also David Spence, who arranged for the excellent photography of the *Granado* model.

My gratitude must also extend to the following: the staff of the Public Record Office at Kew; Tom King of the Ordnance Museum at Priddy's Hard; Dr Schuyler Jones and the staff of the Pitt-Rivers Museum, Oxford; the staff of the Rotunda Artillery Museum at Woolwich; and our Continental friends at the Rigsarkivet, Copenhagen. A special thanks is forwarded to Rob Gardiner and John Franklin for their guidance, and to Anthony J Stirling, who permitted me to borrow his complete volumes of *Model Shipwright*, which provided a wealth of much needed information on various aspects of the subject. Special thanks are also due to Keith Percival for his excellent photographs of the *Granado* model.

Last and most important, I must thank my wife Jan for her dedicated assistance, both in research and in typing my manuscript filled with unfamiliar terminology, and for her overall understanding and patience, for which I am indebted.

Peter Goodwin 1989

ntroduction

THE DEVELOPMENT OF THE BOMB VESSEL

By the seventeenth century large mortars had been used for siege warfare on land for many years; owing, however, to its size, weight and tremendous recoil, the conception of employing such a weapon at sea had never been seriously considered. In comparison to standard ordnance, the mortar had many advantages: its greater range permitted it to be fired from a position well outside the scope of defending artillery, and its projectiles, whether in the form of explosive shells or carcasses (incendiary devices), could be fired at a high trajectory beyond low-lying hills and coastal fortifications. Because sea-going ordnance offered none of these advantages, laying a siege from the sea with conventional armament proved difficult for the attacking fleet.

The idea of using sea mortars was that of the ingenious Basque Bernard Renan D'Elicagaray, who in 1682 introduced a purpose-built ship, the *galiote à bombe*. This vessel, based on the Dutch *galliot*, was short in length and broad in beam, ideal as a stable gun platform. These flute-sterned vessels were given a ketch rig, where the absence of a foremast gave two advantages. First, two mortars could be placed athwartships, before the mainmast; second, it permitted a clear arc of fire ahead. The only disadvantage of this rig was that the sail area was limited. This problem was overcome by increasing the mainmast height and the size of the mainsail, and by enlarging the headsails. On the whole, however, this rig was not satisfactory and often proved unmanageable.

These vessels were first engaged during the French attack on the pirate stronghold of Algiers. This was carried out by Admiral Abraham Duquesne, who sailed from Toulon on 12 July 1682. The action left half the town in flames, all the forts destroyed and over 700 people dead.

The following year the Englishman Edward Dummer (later to become Surveyor of the Navy) witnessed the French carrying out bomb ship trials off Toulon. His observations, recorded in his journal *A Voyage into the Mediterranean*, were later submitted to the Navy Board, and were initially received with the usual reservations by the Lords of the Admiralty. This attitude was soon reversed, for the following year Louis XIV ordered Duquesne to bombard the city of Genoa in retaliation for the Genoese alliance with Spain, Holland and Italy and their involvement with the Barbary Corsairs. The French fleet arrived off Genoa on 6 May 1684 with 8000 troops and presented an ultimatum, which was refused. A continuous bombardment was carried out between 18 and 24 May, during which in excess of 14,000 bombs and incendiaries devastated the entire city. On 28 May a second assault ensued, but the French failed to land troops, ran out of ammunition and subsequently withdrew.

These forays proved that the bomb vessel had given the French Navy supremacy in the Mediterranean. In effect, therefore, an arms race had begun, and after reconsideration the Navy Board ordered that bomb ships should be introduced to the Royal Navy. In 1687 the *Salamander*, built by Robert Lee, was launched at Chatham; this vessel carried two 12¼in brass mortars, eight minions and two faulconettes. Her length was 64ft 4in, breadth 21ft 6in, burthen 134 tons, and she carried a crew of thirty-five.

During the following year a new bomb ship, the *Firedrake*, was launched at Deptford and the yacht *Portsmouth* was converted; both vessels carried two 12¼in brass mortars. A third vessel, the *Helderenberg*, was converted to a bomb tender to carry ammunition, stores and the Royal Artillery personnel employed to fire the mortars. (The Navy employed RA gunners on bomb vessels until 1804.) The *Firedrake* had a gun deck length of 85ft 9in, breadth of 27ft, and a burthen of 279 tons.

These vessels did not prove satisfactory. The Navy Board therefore employed the Frenchman Jean Fournier to supervise forthcoming bomb ship construction. Improved draughts were submitted in 1693, resulting in the building of four purpose-built bomb ships, the *Firedrake*, built at Deptford (the former of the same name being captured), the *Serpent* and *Mortar* at Chatham and the *Granado* (Grenade) at Rotherhithe. A contemporary sketch of the *Mortar* indicates she was ship-rigged, and this suggests that the other ships were also rigged in this fashion. By 1703 three of this build had been lost at sea, and the *Granado* had blown up during action in 1694.

Additional vessels were required during the War of the League of Augsburg (1689–1697). Limited finance and dockyard resources at the beginning of the war necessitated the purchase of eight vessels and their conversion to 'bombs'. All but the *Star*, which remained in service till 1712, were sold off after the Peace of Ryswick.

A second building programme for nine purpose-built vessels commenced in 1695, and all but one of these bombs were built on the Thames. These were the *Basilisk*, *Blast*, *Carcass*, *Comet*, *Dreadful*, *Furnace*, *Thunder*, *Serpent* (Chatham-built) and the *Granado*. The latter two were built 'in the room' of the previous ships of the same name lost in 1694. The last vessel to be built during this century was the *Terror*, built at Limehouse in 1696, which was accidentally lost by fire in 1705. By 1720 only three bombs of the 1695 build remained: the *Basilisk*, *Blast* and *Furnace*. Strictly speaking, no further bombs were built until 1729, but the remaining vessels were supplemented by the hurried conversion of the 20-gun Sixth Rates *Seaford*, *Shoreham* and *Solebay* in 1726 when Spain made preparations to seize Gibraltar.

New draughts were prepared in 1728 to build two bombs. These designs were to form the foundation for all bomb ships constructed during the rest of the eighteenth century. Besides a general increase in length and breadth, much consideration was given to improving the rig; this was achieved by stepping the mainmast further forward. The effect of this modification was twofold. First, more space was provided for the after mortar, thereby giving it a greater arc of fire. Second, the greater part of the sail area could be shifted further forward, and consequently the size of the headsails could be reduced and the mainmast shortened. This innovation also permitted a longer mizzen mast to be fitted. In all, these measures produced a well-balanced rig which improved the overall sailing performance and station-keeping capabilities of the ship. This was essential, for the role of the bomb ship had now become more integrated with that of the fleet as a whole.

Two years later the *Salamander* and the *Terrible* were added to the now depleted bomb list. The former ship, built by Haywood, was launched at Woolwich on 7 July 1730, and the latter a month later on 4 August. The *Terrible*, built by Richard Stacy at Deptford, had a length of 86ft 6in, breadth of 27ft 6in, and a burthen of 262²⁰/₉₄ tons. Unlike previous designs, the draught of the *Terrible* indicates that she was constructed with a small square stern and furnished with a figurehead and trailboards. The quarter deck had also been lengthened and now terminated with a convex bulkhead, a feature that became characteristic on most bombs.

Both these vessels were armed with eight 6-pounders, fourteen swivels and two modified 13in mortars. Prior to this, brass (bronze) mortars set at a fixed angle of 45 degrees had been cast with an integral bedplate. Since the 1690s the French had been using the *trabucco* type mortar, cast with trunnions at its base which permitted variable elevation, an innovation the British had been slow to adopt. Earlier mortars also had no provision for training; the entire ship had to be turned relative to the target. This was achieved by casting anchors ahead and astern and hauling the vessel round on springs set up between the two cables and the windlass. In June 1726 William Ogbourne, Master Carpenter at Woolwich, introduced a new form of mortar bed which both accommodated the *trabucco* type mortar and rotated on a wooden turntable to allow the gun to be aimed without moving the ship.

In 1739 the deterioration of trade relations with Spain resulted with the War of Jenkins's Ear, and this was followed by the War of the Austrian Succession a year later. These two conflicts precipitated a substantial building programme of bomb vessels.

Six ships were ordered on 11 March 1740, all based on the lines of the *Alderney*. Their general dimensions were as follows: length 90ft 6in, keel length 73ft 9in, breadth 26ft, and depth in the hold 11ft. Their burthen was 265¹⁷/₉₄ tons. Unlike previous bombs, this class carried one 13in mortar forward and a 10in mortar aft; this gun was probably a howitzer. This modification in armament was adopted for two reasons. The blast effect of the charge from a smaller mortar greatly reduced the possibility of damage to the main and mizzen shrouds, the relative position of which already imposed restrictions on the after mortar's arc of fire. Second, the howitzer, a far lighter weapon, could, by virtue of its conventionally positioned trunnions, be elevated as required far more easily. These bombs also carried eight 4-pounders and ten swivels and had a complement of sixty men. When converted to sloops, the ships carried an additional two 4-pounders and four swivel guns, and the complement was increased to 100–110 men. The 1740 group is shown in Table 1.

A further six bombs were ordered on 14 September 1741. With modified

TABLE 1: **BOMB VESSELS OF 1740**

Name	Builder	Yard	Keel laid	Launch date	Fate
Basilisk	Snelgrove	Limehouse	3.4.1740	30. 8.1740	Sold 1750
Blast	West	Deptford	19.3.1740	28. 8.1740	Captured by Spanish off Jamaica 19.10.1745
Carcass	Taylor	Rotherhithe	23.4.1740	27. 9.1740	Sold 1749
Furnace	Quallett	Rotherhithe	23.4.1740	25.10.1740	Sold 1763
Lightning	Bird	Rotherhithe	23.4.1740	24.10.1740	Capsized off Leghorn 174
Thunder	Bird	Rotherhithe	23.4.1740	30. 8.1740	Wrecked in hurricane off Jamaica 1744

dimensions the first five vessels were as follows: Length 91ft, keel length 75ft 6in, breadth 26ft, depth in the hold 11ft 3in, and burthen 270 tons. Whether in service as a bomb or a sloop, their armament and complement corresponded to that of the 1740 group, except that two extra swivels were carried. Details of these five ships are shown in Table 2.

TABLE 2: **BOMB VESSELS OF 1741**

Name	Builder	Yard	Keel laid	Launch date	Fate
Comet	Taylor	Rotherhithe	8.10.1741	29.3.1742	Sold 1749
Firedrake	Perry	Blackwall	7.10.1741	20.2.1742	Sold 1763
Mortar	Perry	Blackwall	8.10.1741	25.2.1742	Sold 1749
Serpent	Snelgrove	Limehouse	9.10.1741	15.3.1742	Wrecked 1748
Terror	Greville	Limehouse	9.10.1741	13.3.1742	Sold 1754

The sixth bomb, the *Granado*, built by John Barnard at Ipswich, differed from her contemporaries in that she was constructed with a full square stern. This feature suggests that she was initially intended to be a sloop, but there is no firm evidence to support this theory, especially as the original contract has been lost. Her dimensions were as follows: length 91ft 1in, breadth 26ft 2in, depth in the hold 11ft 4in, draught afore 8ft 9in, abaft 9ft 1in, and burthen 268⁹²/₉₄ tons. The keel was laid on 18 November 1741; she was launched the following year on 22 June, and she remained in service until when she was sold in 1763. This *Granado* is the subject of this book.

After the treaty of Aix-la-Chapelle all of the remaining bombs were to be sold, with the exception of the *Firedrake*, *Furnace* and *Granado*. The only vessels introduced during the subsequent interlude of peace were the converted Sixth Rates *Kingfisher* and *Greyhound* in 1752 and 1755 respectively.

Administrative negligence left the Admiralty unprepared for the unexpected outbreak of the Seven Years War in 1756. To remedy this negligence the *Baltimore*, *Pelican*, *Falcon* and *Racehorse* were hurriedly converted to ship-rigged bombs. In addition, one purpose-built ketch-rigged bomb, the *Infernal* was launched in 1757. Estimates for a further six vessels were forwarded to the Admiralty on 16 October 1758. On 8 January 1759 the Navy Board proposed that three of these vessels were to be rigged with three masts for trials. As noted above, the ketch rig had been improved, but experience had shown that ship-rigged vessels by comparison proved far handier sailers in adverse conditions, especially in confined waters. The ketch-rigged vessels were the *Blast*, built by Bird (Northam), *Thunder*, by Hennicker (Chatham), and *Mortar* by Wells on the Thames; these were the last bombs to be rigged in this fashion. The ship-rigged vessels were the *Basilisk* by Wells (Thames), *Carcass* by Stanton (Thames) and the *Terror* by Barnard at Harwich. All six vessels were armed with one 13in and one 10in mortar, eight 4-pounders and fourteen swivels, and had a complement of sixty men. When converted and used as sloops the ship-rigged vessels carried a total of fourteen 4-pounders and the ketch-rigged ships four extra 4-pounders; all had a complement of 110 men. Their dimensions were as follows: length 91ft 6in, keel length 74ft 1¾in, breadth 27ft 6in, depth in the hold 12ft 1in, and burthen 298²²/₉₄ tons.

Besides the preference for a ship rig, the 1758 design included other modifications. The steering wheel had superseded the less manageable tiller, and the windlass was replaced with one set of riding bitts under the forecastle and a capstan fitted abaft the 10in mortar. Capstans situated on the quarterdeck had been used on some of the earlier bomb ships (see for instance the *Blast*, 1740, draught no. 4313 Box 61), probably specifically for elevating the mortars. The square stern was abandoned in favour of a modified flute stern, which now projected further aft. The head became plainer and most of the elaborate carving was eliminated. The ship-rigged bombs *Aetna* and *Vesuvius*, built in 1776, and the *Terror* and *Thunder* of 1779 were also based on the 1758 design.

During the Napoleonic Wars dockyard capacity was stretched to the limit to maintain the general fleet, which left little room for building smaller craft. In 1797, merchantmen were therefore bought in for conversion to bomb ships; these were the *Explosion, Volcano, Strombola, Hector, Tartarus, Hecla* and *Sulphur*. The dimensions of these vessels varied by a small degree according to the size of the original ship, and a number of inventive modifications were introduced to improve the mortar capabilities, at least on the *Hecla*. Over the next decade the overall dimensions and sizes of the general armament were increased, most vessels being fitted with either 12- or 18-pounders.

These later vessels, the *Vesuvius, Terror* and *Belzebub*, were introduced in 1812. Their dimensions were: length on the range of the deck 102ft, extreme breadth 27ft, moulded breadth 26ft 4in, depth in the hold 13ft, and burthen 325⁷/₉₄ tons.

In 1820 draughts for the *Belzebub, Devastation* and *Volcano* were introduced by Sir Robert Seppings. These were based on those vessels built in 1812, but the 1820 ships were much squarer in cross section, having shallower floors and flat sides. In length they were 105ft on the range of the deck, extreme breadth 28ft 6in, moulded breadth 27ft 10in, depth in the hold 13ft 10in, and burthen 372 tons. Unlike previous designs, Seppings's bombs were constructed with a continuous main deck, a full square stern with quarter galleries and a traditional prow with headrails and figurehead. Their armament consisted of a 13- and a 10in mortar and twelve 18-pounder carronades. The swivel guns previously carried had been dispensed with, as had the sweep ports.

These were the last bomb ships to be built for the Royal Navy, for the developments made in armament during the first half of the nineteenth century dictated a new direction in ship design. Again, the initiative was taken by France, where, under the guidance of Colonel Paixhans, the shell was improved and a shell firing gun was introduced. This innovation eventually led to the introduction of the rifled breech-loader invented by Armstrong in 1855. The explosive shell once fired by a mortar to destroy Morro castle in 1762 now brought the death knell to the old wooden walls and instigated the birth of the ironclad warship. Mortars did however remain in use on small gunboats, especially during the Crimean and the American Civil wars. The concept of the bomb vessel as an individual destructive weapon never completely disappeared; monitors, ships carrying a single large-bore turret gun, were employed to bombard coastal installations during World War II. Fittingly, the last listed mortar ship belonged to the French, a steam sloop which finally went out of service in 1907.

HISTORY

The *Granado* was one of twelve such ships built to supplement the depleted bomb vessel fleet at the outbreak of the War of Jenkins's Ear in 1739, and the ensuing War of the Austrian Succession.

The ship was ordered on 14 September 1741, the contract being given to the reputable Ipswich shipbuilder, John Barnard. The construction work was overseen by the naval Surveyor, Thomas Slade (later to design Nelson's *Victory*). It is now uncertain who actually designed the *Granado*, but Slade's responsibility for the surveying suggests that the design was attributable to him. With regard to design, the *Granado*'s lines indicate that she was originally intended to be a sloop. Unlike contemporary bomb vessels, which were built with a pink stern, the *Granado* was constructed with the more conventional square stern, common to general naval vessels.

The keel was laid on 18 November 1741 and the ship was launched on 22 June the following year (interestingly, her career terminated exactly twenty-one years later). After launching she was taken down river to Harwich, where she was fitted out and put in commission. The Admiralty, however, decided that she was not to take on the role of a bomb vessel and ordered that she be converted to a sloop (Admiralty Order 4 July 1742).

The Captain's Log states the following:

Wednesday, 7th July, 1742; Moored in Harwich Harbour. Put *Granado* Bomb in commission at Harwich/Built at Ipswich and Brought down the 23rd June last to this place; The Caulkers and Carpenters at work on board. There being no men yet entered for the Bomb.

Thursday, 8th July, 1742 . . . An order from the Admty to enter 100 men and fit her as a Sloop for the Channel Service.

From 10 July until 17 August, the ship was rigged, loaded with approximately 60 tons of shingle ballast and stored with provisions for two months. During this period her bomb beds and shell rooms were removed. The Captain's Log notes:

Wednesday, 14th July . . . Rigging, The Carpenters taking down in the Bomb Rooms, Shelves, rollers, and bulkheads. [The exact meaning of the word 'rollers' here is somewhat obscure. The Log is at times almost illegible, so it would seem plausible that the word is actually 'rider', which would make more sense in this context.]

Friday, 16th The Ordinary taking in 15 tons of shingle ballast out of the *Cordelia* Hoy and Mr. Robt. Pervey in loading the said Hoy with the Timber out of the Bomb Rooms to be delivered to the Storekeeper at Harwich.

On 21 August work was completed by bending on the sails, and, 'Surveyed the Stores by order of the Lord of the Admty and put them into the care of Mr. John Skinner, Master'; four days later the *Granado* sailed for Sheerness. Here the ship was put into 'a wett dock' to have the bottom burned, 'and payed it with Tallow'.

On 25 September she sailed from the dockyard on a deployment, operating mainly off the French coast, gathering intelligence and undertaking general policing duties, which continued until 1745. In July of that year it appears that the Admiralty decided to have her reconverted to a bomb vessel (Admiralty

Order 15 July 1745, 'to fit her as a Bomb'; Adm 95/12). This order was, however, reversed two days later and she remained in service as a sloop.

For the next three years the *Granado* was generally employed off the north east coast and East Anglia, intercepting privateers and smugglers. In December 1745 information was received that France was preparing to invade England from Dunkirk. The coastline of Kent and Sussex was already protected by Admiral Vernon's squadron, but the more northerly shores remained unguarded. Commodore Smith at the Nore was therefore instructed to take a small squadron including the *Granado* to cover the Thames estuary and the coasts of Norfolk and Suffolk. His ships were to operate between Gunfleet, Hollesley Bay and Yarmouth Roads 'as you shall think proper' (*The Vernon Papers*, Letter 477 3 December 1745; Navy Records Society vol. 99).

During her docking at Sheerness in June 1747 some modifications were made to the ship internally; 'a platform to be made in wake of the After Hatchway' (Admiralty Order 2 July 1747; Adm 95/12). This improvement was probably undertaken to extend the accommodation spaces below. Initially the intended complement amounted to sixty men, though this number had been increased to 110 when the ship was converted to a sloop.

In 1748 the Peace of Aix-la-Chapelle concluded the War of the Austrian Succession, and *Granado* was therefore paid off and laid up. Peace was not to last long, however; international relations soon began to deteriorate. This and the threat to Britain's interests eventually led to her involvement in what was to become the Seven Years War, a conflict for which the country was ill-prepared. Consequently the *Granado* was taken out of reserve 'to put her in Condition for Service' (Admiralty Order 17 February 1755/56; Adm 180/3). The ship was recommissioned on 26 April 1756.

Three months later the *Granado* was converted for her initial role – 'to fit her at Woolwich for Channel Service as a Bomb Vessel to carry 60 men' (Admiralty Order 26 July, 1756; Adm 180/3).

She remained on Channel service until March 1757, when she was recalled to prepare for her next deployment. The log entry dated 30 March states that while at Limehouse she took on stores: 'Provisioning 8 and 10, 4 pdrs, 100 Bomb Shells, 50 large, 50 small, 16 half barrels of Powder' (Adm 51/413).

The original draught of the *Granado* implies that both mortars were of the same size, but this reference to shell sizes ('50 large, 50 small') suggests that the mortars were indeed 13in and 10in bore respectively. The reference to '8 and 10, 4 pdrs' suggests that at this time *Granado* carried ten 4-pounders, rather than her initial eight. The extra two guns were bow chasers. Although the draught only shows a vague representation of a chase port, alternative draughts indicate these ports more clearly, confirming additional armament.

The following month, under the command of Captain John Fortesque, the *Granado* sailed for Halifax, Nova Scotia, where she arrived on Saturday 6 June 1757. It can be assumed that her orders were to assist with the British assault on the French town of Louisbourg, which guarded the entrance of the St Lawrence river. The capture of this town was essential for the invasion of Canada's interior and the capture of Quebec in 1759. On completion of her task, the ship returned to Portsmouth, arriving home on 11 December.

On 10 October 1758 the *Granado*, now commanded by Captain James Mordale, sailed for the West Indies: it was to be in this theatre of the war that the ship was to play her most active role. On arrival she joined Commodore John Moore's squadron. Moore, with General Hopson, had been ordered to capture the French naval base of Fort Royal, Martinique, this port being of particular importance to France's continental forces in the Mississippi basin and the St Lawrence.

The attack was made in early January 1759, but Moore soon found that his forces were insufficient to lay siege to the formidable fortifications of Fort Royal. An alternative objective, St Pierre, was proposed, but Moore realised that no advantage could be gained by this action; he therefore departed to lay siege to the French citadel of Basse Terre, Gaudeloupe.

The squadron, which included eight ships of the line, anchored off Basse Terre on 22 January 1759. The following morning, after the town had been reconnoitred, the citadel and batteries of Basse Terre were bombarded. The Captain's log reads as follows:

Wednesday, 24th January, 1759 . . . at 2pm Began to Bombarde the Towne and Fort Royal [illegible] the other Bomb ships; The enemy kept a constant Firing at the Bombs and Ships; at 6pm came to with the Bombs in 60 fathom water; Ditto from Fort Royal at One Mile, these Ditto came to with [illegible] our Cable; Ditto kept Constantly Bombarding the Fort and Towne; at 11pm we began to throw Carcasses at the Towne and Sett it on Fire; Ditto kept constantly Bombarding as before. At 9am the Enemy ceased Firing from the Fort. At 11am the Commodore anchored near shore . . .

By Wednesday 24 January the shore batteries had been silenced; troops were then sent ashore to occupy the forts of Basse Terre and Fort Royal. The town itself was devastated by fire caused by the carcasses discharged from the bomb vessels, and much valuable merchandise was lost. On 7 February the fleet turned to Grandterre, the northern part of Gaudeloupe, to attack Fort Louis at the entrance of Cul de Sac Bay.

Wednesday, 7th February, 1759 Fort Royal – 3pm weighed in Company with His Majesties Ships, *Renown* and *Woolwich*, *Infernal* and *Kingfisher* Bombs; at 6 Ditto carried away our Main Topsail Yard in squalls etc. [Note that the *Renown* mentioned here would be the 32-gun ship captured from the French in 1749.]

The assault commenced on the following day, and the log entry reads as follows: 'Thursday, 8th February, 1759 Fort Louis in company with the *Berwick*, *Winchester*, *Roebuck* and *Bonetto* (Sloop); Bombardment commenced after anchoring in 9 fathoms.'

During this action Hopson was killed; Colonel Barrington took command of the army. On Thursday 15 February the bombardment ceased: '. . . at 3pm the Enemy ceased Firing from the Fort and Batteries and sett them on Fire; Our Ships and Bombs ceased Firing; Landed 500 Marines, 100 Highlanders at 8am.'

The next reference indicates the extent to which the recoil of the mortars affected *Granado* herself:

Friday, 16th February, 1759 am. Hauled up our Best Bower Cable and found several of our Punchions of water stove by the Explosions of the Mortar.

Moore left on 13 March, leaving Barrington with one 44-gun ship and the bomb vessels and sloops (including the *Granado*). Smaller engagements continued to break any remaining resistance.

Wednesday, 28th March, 1759 Came to with our Best Bower in 15 fathom water in [illegible] Bay; Ditto from the shore One Cables length; Ditto began to fire our Mortars and Guns to cover the Disembarkation of the Troops at 10. Disembarked all the Troops without any opposition. Ceased Firing our Mortars and Guns.

The *Granado* returned to England in October 1759. After being reconverted to a sloop at Portsmouth (Admiralty Order 20 March 1760) she was deployed in home waters, operating between the Downs, East Anglia, Flushing and

Cuxhaven. The year 1759 had been a successful one, and the course of the war had increasingly favoured Britain. In August 1761 the ship was again converted to a bomb vessel, and she sailed for the West Indies in September. Another attempt to capture Martinique had been planned, and this time sufficient support was to be provided.

On 7 January 1762 Rear Admiral George Rodney's fleet, carrying some 14,000 troops under General Robert Monkton, joined Commodore Sir James Douglas's squadron off Martinique. Although the main offensive commenced a week later, a number of preliminary assaults and feints were planned. The following day, John Morgan, Master of the *Granado*, noted in his log:

Friday, 8th January, 1762 Culdesack Bay Martinique. (near Dimond Rock.)
Saturday, 9th January, 1762 Culdesack Bay – Moderate and Fair Weather – at 5pm some of the Flat Bottom Boats made a feint in the Bay; Do. the Enemy began to Fire Great Guns and Small Armes from Severall partes; Ditto the *Repulse* began to fire; at 6pm the *Basilisk* and *Thunder* Bombs began to throw some Shells; 11 past we got a Spring on our Cable and hove 2 Shells at the Battery of 3 Guns which was firing Abreast of us from the battery – Ceased Firing a.m. Set up the Topmast Rigging. Ditto opened a cask of Irish Beef containing 75 pieces.
Sunday, 10th January, 1762. . . . 2 Shells at Garden Point.
Monday 11th January, 1762. . . . Ditto The *Thunder* fired three shells at the Battery, then it ceased firing.

The main attack started off on 16 January, and the initial bombardment had silenced the shore batteries by noon. Troops were landed in three divisions, which, after meeting stubborn resistance, finally defeated the French on the 27th, though the island did not fall entirely to Britain until 16 February.

Shortly afterwards, Spain allied herself to France (the so-called Family Compact) and declared war on Britain. To subdue possible Spanish aggression in the West Indies, Britain made preparations to attack and capture Havana.

A large fleet was assembled, commanded by Admiral Sir George Pocock and Commodore Augustus Keppel. On 5 March 1762 this fleet sailed from England, carrying with it a large military force under the Earl of Albemarle. Naval vessels already in the West Indies were deployed to support Pocock, and this included *Granado*. Pocock arrived off Havana on 5 June, and the expeditionary force was landed the following day. Havana was primarily defended from La Cabana ridge and El Morro castle; the batteries of the latter guarded the narrow harbour entrance. Two vessels had also been sunk at this entrance to protect the fifteen Spanish warships and 100 merchantmen within. The siege continued for over two months. On 17 July, *Granado*'s log states:

Morro Castle; 7pm Troops opened a Mortar and a Gun battery against Morro aback of it and kept an incessant Fire the whole night as did our Bomb Battery to the northward of the Morro when the Fire became brisk on both sides, at 8pm perceived the *Cambridge*, *Dragon* and *Malborough* bearing down towards the Morro; at 9 the Enemy began to fire at the ships mentioned from the Castle and Point Battery which the *Cambridge* returned soon after; at ¼ past 9 the *Cambridge* brought her broadside to beare on the Castle; ½ past the *Dragon* and *Malborough* came to when a general cannonade ensued from the ships, Castle and Battery on shore also the *Dragon* made the *Stirling Castle* Signal for her Captain at noon, The fire from all sides continued extremely hot, came in the *Dublin* and *Glasgow* Men of War with 2 Spanish Prizes.

On 30 July El Morro finally surrendered, after suffering considerable losses including that of the gallant Commandant, Luis Vicente de Valesco. Meanwhile, Albemarle's troops had been sadly depleted by malaria and dysentery.

However, he was soon reinforced by fresh divisions from Yorktown, and Havana eventually capitulated on 13 August 1762.

It appears that during this campaign the *Granado*'s commander, Captain Stair Douglas, was transferred to the sloop *Port Royal* (14), and the first lieutenant was left to command the *Granado*. It is a reasonable assumption that Captain Stair Douglas's son of the same name commanded the 74-gun ship *Bellona* between 1808 and 1812 (see the *Anatomy of the 74-gun Ship Bellona*, Brian Lavery, Conway Maritime Press, 1985.)

The *Granado* remained in the West Indies, finally sailing for England on Tuesday 7 April 1763. She arrived at Spithead on Sunday 29 May and moved to Woolwich a week later to pay off. The Master, John Hindes, made his last entry in the log:

Wednesday, 22nd June, 1763 Mod and Cloudy, at ½ past 8am Struck the Pendant.

The Captain's last entry follows:

Thursday, 23rd June, 1763 Landed the Men and Paid her Off.

The ship was surveyed afloat on 6 July and 'found to want large repair'. The following day it was proposed that she be sold with her stores, and this act was officially authorised by the Admiralty on 20 July. On 30 August 1763 the *Granado* was sold, for £575. Her career ended with the close of the Seven Years War.

TABLE 3: **CAPTAINS OF THE GRANADO**

Name	From	To
Thomas Elliott	7 July 1742	19 November 1742
Arthur Upton	20 November 1742	7 January 1743
William Parry	8 January 1743	3 October 1744
William Thomas	13 November 1744	June 1746
John Evans	June 1746	12 September 1746[1]
Cornelius Snell	17 August 1747	10 April 1748
Matthew Moore	25 April 1755[2]	23 May 1756
John Fortesque	24 August 1756	14 October 1757
James Mordale	20 January 1758	17 December 1760
John Botterall	23 February 1760	23 February 1761
Stair Douglas	27 March 1762	1 July 1762
Thomas Fraser	2 July 1762	23 June 1763

1. Captain John Evans appears to have relieved Captain William Thomas for the months June, July, August and part of September of 1746. The log has a termination signature by William Thomas.
2. The ship was out of commission between 1748 and 1755.

Battle honours of the *Granado*

1759	Attack on Martinique	1762	Capture of Martinique
1759	Capture of Gaudeloupe	1762	The Havana expedition

CONSTRUCTION

At this period most men-of-war were constructed to the specifications authorised by the Navy Board in the Establishment List of 1741. This directive was an amendment of the preceding Establishments of 1719 and 1733. These rules, however, did not apply to bomb ship construction; these vessels were generally built by contract, a practice which had applied to all naval construction prior to the introduction of the first Establishment in 1706.

Unfortunately, the contract given to John Barnard for building the *Granado* has been lost. This document would have presented us with a detailed list of the specifications and timber dimensions necessary for her construction. These instructions, however, were only a guide (albeit a firm one) for the constructor, who in practice would use his discretion to interpret the Navy Board's requirement. This does not imply that he deviated greatly from the rules, rather that he would apply a more practical approach in order, for example, to reduce timber wastage.

Traditional ship-building timbers were employed for the *Granado*. The keel, made from elm, was actually made in four lengths, each section being vertically scarphed and the sections bolted together. Elm was chosen for its durability when immersed in seawater for long periods and its irregular grain pattern (which permitted it to receive numerous bolts without splitting). Rising vertically at the after end of the keel were the sternpost and its supporting inner post, both made from oak. Each of these timbers was fashioned with a tenon at the heel, which located with a corresponding mortice cut into the keel. Further support was achieved by means of the deadwood, a series of timbers forming a bracket upon the keel. Similarly, at the fore end of the keel the stempost and its supporting false post (apron) were erected. These timbers were made from pieces of 'compass' oak, scarphed and bolted together. The heel of the stempost was joined to the keel by means of an intricate joint termed the 'boxing'; the false post extended into the fore deadwood. Next the hog (or rising wood), also of oak, was laid longitudinally along the top of the keel; its upper surface was scored to receive the floor timbers of the frames. The hog extended to the deadwood at either end, to allow the desired rise of the floors.

In comparison with that of similar-sized naval ships, the construction of bomb vessels had to be extremely strong, to withstand the forces imposed by the violent recoil of the mortars. Current theories on the method and disposition of framing in naval vessels at this period are inconclusive, and since circa 1715 the framing systems employed had, in some respects, undergone considerable modification.

All naval draughts for this period indicate station lines at every third position (ie A, D, E etc, or 4, 7, 10 etc). In the case of the *Granado* these intervals are spaced at 6ft, which, when divided by three, produces a 'room and space' of 2ft. The fore and aft siding of each floor timber was 11in and for each first futtock, 10½in, the sum of which gives a 'room' of 21½in and a space of 2½in. This latter dimension leaves little room for the adoption of the conventional frame systems used after circa 1760, so only two plausible methods for disposing the ship's frames or timbers could have been used.

The first method would involve the ship being built entirely of 'double' or main frames throughout, the joint or station lines being disposed 2ft apart. While this system appears suitable, especially when strength was at a premium, it does not, however, seem likely to have been used. The second system, more probably employed, consisted of double or main frames disposed at every third station (every 6ft as indicated on the draught) with three single filling frames evenly disposed between. Two forms of single frames were alternated between the main frames. This method proves similar to the one double and two single frame system used later, when station lines were indicated at every second room and space on draughts after circa 1760.

The main frames were made up in two 'slices', one half being made up of a floor, second futtock and toptimber, the other half, a first futtock, third futtock and toptimber (lengthening piece). The smaller ships of this period were not fitted with fourth futtocks, but it can be assumed that some builders may have included them in order to reduce timber wastage or when suitable compass oak could not be procured. When these components had been assembled to form each half of the full frame, the two halves were fayed and bolted together at the joint line.

The square frames extended between station 16 aft and N forward; beyond these points cant frames were fitted. These cant frames were fayed and bolted directly onto the side of the deadwood. The angle at which each was set corresponded to the related curvature of the ship's hull as it diminished towards the centreline each end of the vessel; the greatest angle did not exceed 45 degrees. The aftermost cant (20), known as the fashion piece, supported the extremities of the wing transom. Beyond the foremost cant (S) a series of hawse timbers and bollard timbers formed the structure of the bow.

Once all the frames had been set up in position the whole structure was locked rigid by a series of longitudinal members. The first and most important of these was the keelson, which ran fore and aft along the centreline, directly above the keel. The fore end of the keelson continued up the after face of the apron, at which point it was generally referred to as the stemson. At the after end the keelson was married into a large knee called the sternson, which gave additional support to the sternpost.

Adjacent to the keelson was a longitudinal known as the limberstrake, which acted as a clamp to hold the floor timbers. The planking covering the floors of the hold was known as the footwaling and the ceiling.

Next to be fitted was the 'thickstuff'. This comprised a series of bands of heavy planking laid over the inner faces of the frame at varying levels which corresponded to the joint lines of the floors and various futtocks. The upper strakes of the thickstuff wrought over the third futtock heads were scored to receive the ends of the mortar pit beams. In a similar fashion the deck clamps which supported the beam ends were wrought at their respective deck levels.

The deck beams greatly enhanced the strength of the ship in its transverse plane. Most of the beams fitted in the midship section were fashioned from two lengths of pitch pine scarphed and bolted together, those fitted afore and abaft being short enough to be made out of a single timber. The ends of the beams were supported vertically with hanging knees and horizontally with lodging knees. The timber from which they were made was carefully selected, or even grown to shape, to ensure that the grain curvature gave the maximum strength required. The beams of the fore and after platforms were not supported by hanging or lodging knees; their ends were simply shaped to fit and bolted.

Worked intercostally between the beams were a series of lighter timbers called carlings and ledges. The carlings were laid longitudinally in two tiers, the innermost forming the boundaries of the hatchways and so on. The ledges were worked transversely between the tiers of carlings, usually three between each deck beam. Carlings and ledges were only fitted on the upper deck.

The bottom planking of the ship was between 2 and 3in thick, the thicker boards forming the diminishing strakes below the mainwale. Due to the complex hull shape at the fore and after ends, stealers and drop strakes were worked to prevent the boards 'snying'. The ends of the planks, which were set into the rabbets of the stem and stern posts, were called hood ends. The mainwales were wrought in two strakes of oak 4in thick and 10in deep, with a filling strake wrought between them. The planking of the mainwale was joined together by 'hook and butt' scarphs. The function of this heavily-built wale was to bind the hull longitudinally to resist the hogging and sagging stresses which afflicted wooden ships of this era. The rest of the ship's side was planked up with 2in boards.

Internally, waterways were worked along the side of the ship over the outboard ends of the beams; these formed a watertight seal between the deck and the ship's side. Above each waterway a thick band of planking called the pirketting was worked up to the level of the gunport sills. The spirketting was usually wrought in the 'top and butt' fashion. The remaining space was planked up with relatively thin planking known as the lining or quickwork.

The framing of the stern consisted of a series of counter timbers which were set up and bolted at their heels to the wing transom, which supported the whole of the stern structure above the stern post. The counter timbers were braced laterally with deck transoms and transom beams, and planked up with 2in boards. At the fore part of the hull the structure was stiffened with deck hooks and breast hooks, wrought across the inboard side of the hawse pieces.

Each shell room and its related mortar pit formed an integral part of the ship's structure. Therefore, oak of considerable scantling was used for their construction. This was necessary as these assemblies both supported the weight of the mortars and absorbed their violent recoil. The entire structure was built upon five oak floor riders which fitted across the keelson. These timbers were extended up the ship's side with futtock riders, which terminated just below the mortar pit beams. The shell room construction itself comprised six longitudinal beams, three at the base and three at the top. Between these, eighteen square pillars were erected, each fashioned with a tenon at the head and the heel, which fitted into mortices cut into the longitudinal beams. Two tiers of racks on which the shells were kited (stored) were fitted between the pillars. The sides of the shell room were planked up with oak boards 2in thick. Access was obtained by two heavy doors fitted at the end of the room nearest the main hatchway.

The mortar pit was supported by six oak transverse beams fitted over the shell room, the centre two being set together directly below the mortar. Over these, two layers of deck planking were laid, each plank being 'cyphered' edge-to-edge to prevent water ingress. The upper layer of planks was cut to form a circular recess for the mortar bed turntable, which rotated about an iron spindle let into the lower layer of planking. The sides of the pit were built up with trimmer beams, planks and chocks to form an octagonal well in the upper deck. A rectangular housing, consisting of portable sections which could be dismantled, enclosed the mortar. This housing was furnished with two sliding canopies. The remaining area of the pit either side was closed in with removable covers.

DECORATION

Very few bomb ships were embellished with elaborate carvings at the head or stern. The *Granado*, however, was an exception, and the degree to which she was decorated tends to confirm that she was initially intended for use as a sloop.

Her figurehead was of the Greek god Hermes adorned with his characteristic winged helmet. In the god's right hand was a mortar bomb, in the left a winged sceptre. The trailboards were embellished with dolphins and sea serpents. The head rails, timbers and hair bracket were fashioned with relatively plain mouldings. The ends of the catheads bore the traditional lion's head.

The decoration of the quarter badges consisted of fluted pillars (for the window mullions) scrolls and foliage surmounted by the Georgian crown. The light sill of the badge was supported by a phoenix in full flight. The quarter figures, carved in the fashion of Roman legionnaires, also carried mortar bombs. The finishing below these figures bore carvings of mythical creatures which appear to be half fish and half reptile.

At the stern the five lights were divided by fluted and panelled pillars; above these the cove was fashioned with a floral and foliage design. At the centre of the tafferal was another bomb, with arms, trumpets and flags extending from the central point. To each side is a classical figure in a reclining attitude, each

carrying a bomb in one hand. Fire breathing dragons with coiled serpentlike bodies finish the facade at each quarter.

INTERNAL ARRANGEMENT

In relation to other vessels employed in naval service, the layout of the *Granado* was very simple but rather cramped. A considerable portion of the ship was taken up by the mortars and their respective shell rooms, leaving little space for the accommodation of the crew. This problem was somewhat alleviated by the fact that the personnel actually engaged in firing the mortars consisted of a contingent of Royal Artillery men who generally accompanied the *Granado* aboard a bomb tender vessel.

The *Granado* was built without any full-length decks, the upper deck being stepped down aft to maximise the cabin accommodation below the quarter-deck. At the fore end of the ship was a short forecastle which served as an 'anchor' deck. Below the upper deck the ship consisted of little more than the hold with platforms fitted at the fore and after ends. The remaining space was taken up by the two shell rooms, the pump well and the cable tier.

The fore platform extended from the fore side of the forward shell room to the fore peak. The midship section consisted of the galley and its firehearth, with a small separate lobby aft accommodating a companionway to the upper deck. The port side of the platform was divided off into two compartments, the boatswain's cabin aft and the sailroom forward. The opposite side of the platform was similarly divided for the carpenter's cabin, with his storeroom adjacent forward. The fore peak was used as the boatswain's storeroom, housing mainly cordage, blocks and tackle. The space below the platform was divided into two storerooms for provisions, with access to one from the galley and to the other from the lobby.

The after platform consisted of two separate deck levels. The after part formed both the filling room and the magazine. Between these two compartments was a small square room which served as the lightroom for both. Access to the magazine was via the filling room, from the lobby on the other deck level forward. Access to the lightroom was from the same lobby, since safety precluded a direct connection between lightroom and magazine.

The fore part of the after platform was divided into two cabins each side of the ship, with a central lobby. These cabins served for the surgeon, purser, and two other officers holding the King's Warrant. Below the lobby were the captain's store, steward's room and the spirit room, access being via a centreline hatchway on the deck above. Aft of the magazine, the remaining space served as the breadroom. Forward of the after platform was the step for the mizzen mast, either side of which passed the vertical casings of two of the ship's four elm tree pumps. These two pumps served to provide water for washing down decks and firefighting, taking a direct suction from the sea. During the actual firing of the mortars all the decks and bulkheads of the ship were wetted down as an anti-flash precaution.

With the exception of the shell rooms, the remaining area of the hold was given over to the stowage of provisions. Between the two shell rooms at the centreline was the step for the mainmast, and the pump well. To remove water from the well, and ultimately, from the bilges, two further elm tree pumps were fitted here. They were operated from the upper deck, to which they discharged overboard via leather hoses. Either side of the well were the cable tiers, where the anchor cables were stowed and allowed to drain off into the bilges when not in use.

The two shell rooms occupied the spaces before and abaft the mainmast step. Each of these rooms served to house a ready-use supply of shell, but, because of their robust construction, they also supported the mortars with their respective beds.

The upper deck remained flush to a point a little abaft the mizzen mast, where it terminated at a bulkhead which divided off the after cabin accommodation and also formed the break of the quarter deck. Either side of the mizzen mast were the heads of the two elm tree pumps employed for washing down decks. Before the mast was the after mortar, the smaller of the two. The fitting of both mortars, with their beds, pits and covers, is discussed below.

Between the two mortars was the mainmast, with its associated topsail sheet bitts and jeer bitts, and, at each side, the heads of the two bilge pumps with their brake handles. Abaft the mainmast was the main hatchway, used for the embarkation of stores and provisions. It also served for the passage of shell from the shell rooms to the mortars during action.

Forward of the mainmast was the 13in mortar, with its bed and pit. A fore hatchway occupied the area to the fore side of the mortar. This gave access to the fore platform and, like the main hatch, was used for the conveyance of shells during an engagement. To each side of this hatch a spanshackle for the fish davit was fastened to the deck.

Unlike later bomb ketches, the Granado was not furnished with a capstan, but fitted with a windlass, a little abaft the break of the forecastle. The windlass spindle was supported by two carrick bitts, which also served as riding bitts when the vessel was at anchor. The heels of the carrick bitts extended to the ceiling of the hold, thus giving maximum support when employed as riding bitts. The timbers were secured to adjacent deck beams for further support. To further alleviate the stresses imposed as the ship rode at anchor, each carrick bitt was additionally supported with a standard extending over a number of beams forward under the forecastle. Passing through the deck between the two standards was the galley firehearth flue, which terminated on the forecastle.

Between the forecastle and the quarterdeck the bulwarks were pierced with five gunports each side for the small carriage guns used to defend the ship against gunboats, cutters, etc. The bulwarks were also pierced for nine sweep ports a side, arranged in four pairs between the gunports, with the ninth abaft the fifth gunport. The sweeps were employed both for manoeuvring the ship when becalmed or in light winds, and to make minor adjustments to the vessel's position while carrying our a bombardment.

The after end of the upper deck was stepped down to form the after cabin space. Access to the accommodation was by a door fitted on the port side of the bulkhead. The cabin space was divided into two separate cabins each side of a central lobby. These cabins were allocated to the master and the lieutenant.

The remaining space, abaft a transverse bulkhead, comprised the captain's accommodation, which was subdivided into a day cabin and a bedplace. The day cabin was illuminated by both the quarter badge lights and stern lights. Further ventilation to the cabin spaces was through two gunports each side, though it is doubtful if any guns were ever carried at these positions.

The quarterdeck was primarily used for the navigation of the vessel. Unlike the later bomb ketches of the late 1750s, Granado was not fitted with a steering wheel; she was steered by tiller only. The rudder head passed through the captain's quarters, terminating within a boxlike housing on the quarterdeck. The fore side of the housing was open to receive the tiller.

The forecastle was relatively short in length and sufficed as an anchor deck. The heels of the catheads, from which the anchors were suspended when not in use, terminated upon the forecastle deck. At the after end, midships, was the belfry with its plain arched canopy supported by two pillars terminating on the

upper deck, and secured to the aftermost forecastle beam.

The Granado and her class were all built with a square stern and an ornate head. These features were unusual and are found only on those vessels built during the 1740–42 building programme.

STEERING GEAR

The Granado was steered by means of a rudder and tiller; a steering wheel was thought unnecessary for a ship of this size. The rudder was made from three pieces of timber, the main piece of which extended the entire length of the rudder. Two separate baulks of timber were fayed and bolted to the after face of the main piece, thereby increasing the overall working surface. These pieces differed in length and formed a series of steps or hances at the back edge of the rudder. To the heel of the rudder a sole piece was fitted, to prevent damage to the endgrain of the rudder itself; this was generally made from elm.

The rudder was suspended from the stern post by four pairs of pintles and gudgeons. The gudgeons were wrought integral with braces, which were bolted to the hull, and similar braces were formed with the pintles to give additional stiffening to the rudder itself.

The main piece, or rudder stock, extended upward through the helm port in the lower counter, through the captain's accommodation, and terminated about 18in above the level of the quarterdeck. The head of the rudder stock was fashioned with a mortice to receive the after end of the tiller. The timber at this point was strengthened with a number of iron hoops and straps to prevent splitting. The complete rudder head was enclosed in a box-form housing, the fore face of which remained open to admit the tiller.

The tiller was made from ash, a wood chosen for its inherent flexibility. The after end of the tiller was completed with a tenon, which fitted into the mortice in the rudder head. The opposing end was formed into a curved handle for the helmsman. Under normal conditions only one helmsman would have steered the vessel, though assistance would have been necessary during heavy weather.

GROUND TACKLE

The Granado probably carried three bower anchors, one stream and one kedge anchor. Alternatively, she may have had a sheet anchor in place of one bower anchor; it is also possible that due to the nature of her role a spare kedge anchor may have been carried. The various weights of the anchors suitable for this size of vessel were as follows: bower 20cwt, (sheet 18cwt), stream 7½cwt, and kedge 3½cwt. All the anchors were made of wrought iron. Each was furnished with a wooden stock made in two halves, joined together with bolts and iron hoops. The function of the stock was to 'trip' the anchor, thereby allowing one of the palms to embed itself in the seabed. Two of the bower anchors were secured at all time to their respective cables, ready for instant use. Each was stowed, suspended from its cathead and lashed to the ship's side. The third bower (or sheet) anchor was secured abaft the starboard bower, free of its cable. The stream anchor was generally stowed below, while the kedge anchor was lashed to the spare bower.

A ship of this size generally carried six cables, all of which were 120 fathoms in length. Five of these cables were of 13in circumference, two for the bower anchors and three spare. The sixth cable, of 8in circumference, was primarily used for the kedge anchor, since its lighter weight permitted easier transportation, especially when warping the ship. The cable passed in through a hawse hole at the bow of the ship and then passed to the windlass, around which it was turned; it was then carried aft to the main hatchway, where it descended into the cable tier.

The windlass consisted of two stout vertical timbers called carrick bitts, which supported the horizontal windlass spindle. The spindle was further retained by removable cheeks which were forelocked to the bitts. The windlass was rotated by means of wooden handspikes, which were inserted in the square sockets disposed radially around the spindle. Warping heads for hauling lesser cables were fashioned at each end of the spindle. Iron pawls fitted to the belfry stanchions slotted into the two pawl rings near the centre of the spindle, thus acting as a ratchet to prevent the spindle reversing direction when hauling. Disengagement of the pawls permitted the windlass to veer and the cable to run freely. The carrick bitts were supported on their fore side by long standards, so that the whole assembly acted as a pair of riding bitts when the ship was at anchor. The windlass also served to hoist the yards, raise the mortars and embark stores, etc, and the ship's boats.

When the anchor was being weighed, the windlass was operated by ten to twelve men. When the anchor broke surface the catblock was lowered from the cathead and hooked to the anchor ring, and the anchor was then hoisted vertically to the cathead, or 'catted', as the operation was known. Next the fish davit, with its fish block, was hoisted out over the ship's side, its inboard end being retained by the spanshackle fitted on the opposite side of the ship. The anchor was then 'fished' by means of the fish block hook and hoisted to a horizontal position, then lashed in place. The ship's side was protected from the anchor flukes by the anchor lining.

PUMPS
The *Granado* was furnished with four elm tree pumps, two of which were used for the removal of water from the bilges and the pump well, and two for washing down decks, firefighting and other domestic requirements. These two differed from the first pair in that each pump took a direct suction from the sea, the lower part of the casing passing through the bottom of the ship.

Each pump, regardless of its function, was constructed in the same manner. The pump casing was made from elm, bored out parallel to its entire length and shaped to the desired external diameter. The complete casing was reinforced with a series of iron hoops which were shrunk onto the timber when the wood was dry. Two pistons or 'boxes' were fitted within the tube of the pump, one of which was fixed the other free to reciprocate. The lower box, which can be regarded as that which was fixed, was in fact set a short distance from the lower part of the casing, and was actually retained in position by its own weight and its interference fit with the wood as the timber swelled when wet. The complete box was fitted with a non-return valve, often referred to as a poppet valve, and an iron staple. The latter was fitted to allow the box to be retrieved by a hook for inspection and maintenance.

The upper box was manufactured in the same manner as the lower box, with the exception that it was free to move within the casing. An iron shaft known as the spear was attached to the staple of this box. The upper end of the spear was loose fitted to the operating handle, or 'brake', and the brake was allowed to pivot on a pin set between two 'ears'. The ears were made integral with the uppermost iron hoop.

Operation of the pump was simple, though not particularly efficient; the output was approximately 25 gallons per minute. The action of the pump was as follows. When the brake was operated to lower the upper valve box, the water between the two boxes was compressed until the non-return valve on the upper box lifted, allowing water to pass from below to above the box. The same compressive action kept shut the valve on the lower, fixed box. On the upward movement of the free box the water above it was lifted to the discharge pipe, fitted at the top of the casing. At the same time a partial vacuum occurred between the two valve boxes, thus allowing the poppet valve on the lower box to lift and admit water to the casing. The valve shut again on the next downward movement, thereby continuing the action of the pump.

Leather hoses were fastened to the pump discharge pipe when in use. The hoses were led either to the ship's side, or to the scuppers when pumping out the bilges, or directed as necessary when employed with the domestic pumps.

ARMAMENT
The *Granado* was equipped with three types of ordnance: 4-pounder carriage guns, half-pounder swivel guns and two large sea mortars.

Initially eight 4-pounders were carried, but this number was increased to ten after the ship's conversion to a sloop, with the additional guns placed either under the forecastle as bow chasers or at the fifth gunports. Each gun was 6ft long (excluding the cascable), with a bore of 3.7in (including windage), and weighed 2cwt 2qtrs 13lb. The solid iron round shot had a diameter of 3½in. Maximum range for the 4-pounder was approximately 1700 yards, and point blank range, 300 yards. The charge required to fire a 4-pound shot was between one third and one half of the weight of the shot (1½–2lb). Other charges required were as follows: proof firing 4lb, saluting 2lb, and scaling 6oz. The latter amount was used as an increment to attain variations between point blank and maximum range. The standard gun crew consisted of four men.

The gun itself was mounted on a conventional carriage made of elm. This timber was suitable for two reasons: first, it did not fragment into small dangerous splinters when damaged by shot (a hazzard to personnel), and second, it withstood the shock of the gun's recoil. The carriage consisted of two side cheeks, a front transom and a bed, which carried the quoin. The quoin was a wedge-shaped block of timber placed under the breech and was used to elevate or depress the gun as required. Axeltrees made from elm were fitted at the fore and after ends of the carriage, onto which trucks (wooden wheels) of oak were fitted. These could be removed if necessary; the removal of the rear trucks gave greater elevation to the gun. The gun barrel was held to the carriage by iron hinges known as cap squares, which fitted over the trunnions and were locked down by a pin inserted in the keep plate.

Each gun was furnished with gun tackle, traversing tackle and a breeching rope. The breeching was a good-quality stout hemp rope which secured the gun to the bulwark and took the strain of the recoil. Its inboard end was passed around the cascable behind the breech of the gun. Fitted either side of the carriage was the gun tackle, which was used to run the gun out ready to fire. At the rear of the carriage was the traversing tackle. This served two functions; one was simply to haul the gun back for reloading, and the other was to make oblique fire possible, by transferring the tackle to an adjacent ringbolt in the deck. In addition, the ship may have had four extra guns carried on the after accommodation deck, as did the *Furnace* of 1742.

It is stated that twelve half-pound guns were carried on the ship; this figure can be disputed, for there were altogether eighteen mounting pedestals. These guns were used primarily as anti-personnel weapons, and could be loaded with cannister shot as an alternative to a single round. Each gun was 3ft long, weighed approximately 2cwt, and had a bore diameter of 1½in. The diameter of the solid shot was approximately 1¼in. The charge required to fire a half-pound ball was 3oz, proof 8oz, saluting 3oz and scaling 1oz. The gun was mounted by its trunnions into an iron yoke furnished with a pintle, which was inserted into a vertical hole bored into the timber pedestal. These pedestals were bolted along the ship's side, with eight on the quarterdeck, four at the waist and six on the forecastle.

The two sea mortars were fitted on the centreline, one before and one abaft the mainmast. Initially the *Granado* carried two 13in mortars, but the after mortar was later replaced with a mortar of 10in calibre, which in all probability took the form of a howitzer.

The 13in mortars indicated on the draught were 5ft 3in long overall and weighed 4 tons 1cwt 1qtr 18lb. This type of ordnance was cast in bronze and designed with two chambers, one of 13in bore to receive the shell, the other of 8in bore for the charge. Two large trunnions to permit the gun to be secured to the bed and to elevate the piece were integrally cast at the base of the breech; this design was known as the *trabucco* mortar.

The mortar was mounted by its trunnions onto the bed, with the trunnions retained by heavy iron cap squares, eyebolts and locking pins. The bed itself was made from heavy baulks of oak fayed and strongly bolted together to withstand the recoil forces incurred. The bed was designed with a recess to permit the mortar to be housed in the horizontal position when not in use. The entire assembly was bolted to an oak turntable, which was set down into the mortar pit deck. The turntable itself rotated about a stout iron spindle, thereby enabling the gun to be trained on its target. When required, the mortar was initially elevated by means of a strop passed around the muzzle and lifting tackle suspended from the masthead. Once raised, the mortar was supported by an iron chock set at 45 degrees, the chock being retained with forelock bolts.

The maximum range with the mortar elevated at 45 degrees was 4100 yards. The charge required to fire the shell was approximately 32lb, though this amount of powder was seldom used, due to the violent recoil and subsequent stress imposed to the ship's hull. In practice a reduced charge of between 12 and 15lb was generally used. The proof firing charge was 30lb.

The hollow spherical shell fired by the mortar was approximately 12½in in diameter, and weighed 197lb when empty. This size of shell gave a clearance of ¼in either side for windage. The wall of the shell at its base was 3in thick, diminishing to 2in at the top next to the fuse hole. The greater thickness at the base ensured that the shell withstood the pressure of the firing charge and that it landed correctly on impact, thus protecting the fuse. Two iron lugs to facilitate transportation and loading were forged onto the top of the shell.

When charged, the cavity of the shell was filled with 10lb 4oz of powder; the size of the charge was generally rated at two thirds of the cavity capacity. The fuse consisted of a hollow conical tube made from either beech or willow, filled with a preparation of saltpetre, sulphur and finely ground powder. The external surface of the fuse was graduated with scores around its periphery, each line representing half a second of burning time. The fuse length would be cut accordingly, depending on the trajectory and range of the target, thus ensuring that the shell exploded on impact. The fuse was then driven into the fusehole with a mallet and sealed with tallow mixed with beeswax or pitch. Once inserted, the shell was said to be 'fixed' (charged), and the sealing was removed when required.

The 10in mortar of this period was 4ft 8in in length and weighed 38cwt 2qtr 14lb. Its maximum range was 4000 yards when elevated at 45 degrees. The charge required to fire the shell this distance was approximately 6lb 4oz, the scaling charge 4oz and proof firing charge 12lb 8oz. The shell, which weighed 93lb when empty, had a diameter of 9.8in, and when 'fixed' it held a charge of 4lb 5oz. The manner in which this mortar was mounted and the bed design were identical to that of its 13in counterpart.

Details of the 10in howitzers employed in the mid-eighteenth century are

TABLE 4: **DETAILS OF 13in SEA MORTARS**

Type	Weight of Piece			Length of Piece		Weight of Shell when empty	Range at 45 degrees	Charge of powder required							
								Proof		Firing	Shell charge		Scalin	
	cwt	qtr	lb	ft	in	lb	yd	lb	oz	lb	lb	oz	lb	oz
Brass*	88	2	6	5	3	197	4100	30	0	12–15	10	4		8
Brass*	87	0	10	5	3	197	4100	30	0	12–15	10	4		8
Brass*	86	0	0	5	3	197	4100	30	0	12–15	10	4		8
Iron	82	2	0	5	2	200	4000	?		?	10	4		8
Brass*	82	0	0	5	3	197	4100	30	0	12–15	10	4		8
Brass*	81	2	24	5	3	197	4100	30	0	12–15	10	4		8
Brass*	81	1	18	5	3	197	4100	30	0	12–15	10	4		8
Iron	36	0	0	3	7	200	1800	8	8	3–4	10	4		8
Iron	36	0	0	3	5	200	1800	8	8	3–4	10	4		8
Iron	30	0	0	4	4	197	1800	8	8	3–4	10	4		8
Iron	25	0	0	3	7	197	1600	8	8	3–4	10	4		8

* Brass – Bronze

TABLE 5: **DETAILS OF 10in MORTARS**

Type	Weight of Piece			Length of Piece		Weight of Shell when empty	Range at 45 degrees	Charge of powder required							
								Proof		Firing		Shell charge		Scalin
	cwt	qtr	lb	ft	in	lb	yd	lb	oz	lb	oz	lb	oz	lb	oz
Iron	41	0	0	4	8	92	4000	3	4			5	5		
Brass*	38	0	14				4000	12	8						
Brass*	34	8	26	4	8		4000	12	8						
	34	0	0				4000	12	8						
Brass*	33	0	0	4	8	93	3809	12	8			4	5		4
Brass*	32	3	7	4	8	93	3809	12	8			4	5		4
Brass*	32	2	20	4	4	93	3809	12	8			4	5		4
Iron	16	0	0	2	9	92	1600	3	4	2	2	5	5		4
Brass*	9	3	27	2	9		1600	3	4	2	2	4	5		4
Iron				3	9		1600	3	4	2	2	4	5		4

* Brass – Bronze

somewhat scarce. This weapon had two advantages over the mortar: not only was it lighter in weight, it was also cast with the trunnions midway along th barrel length, which permitted the gun to be elevated far more easily. Th howitzer of this calibre fitted aboard naval ships was approximately 5ft i length and weighed between 10 and 12cwt. The size of the shell, the variou charges and range were identical to those given above for the 10in mortar. Th bed itself was considerably smaller in construction, while the mountin arrangements were, because of the trunnion positions, similar to those used o conventional carriage guns.

As an alternative to explosive shells, incendiary devices known as 'carcasses were fired from the mortars. These consisted of a projectile made in the form o an iron cage 1ft ½in in diameter by 1ft 4in long, weighing 44lb. The interior o the carcass was filled with inflammable materials, which were ignited by th firing charge. One contemporary description of this missile in the *1750 Guide* i as follows: 'A Carcass, which they fill at Sieges with Pitch, Tar and othe Combustables, to set Towns on Fire: It is thrown out of an 18 Inch Mortar an will burn two Hours where it happens to fall'. Very little imagination i required to appreciate the destructive effect of bombardment with thes incendiary devices.

TABLE 6: DETAILS OF 10in HOWITZERS

Type	Weight of Piece			Length of Piece		Weight of Shell when empty	Range at 45 degrees	Charge of powder required					
								Proof		Firing	Shell charge		Scaling
	cwt	qtr	lb	ft	in	lb	yd	lb	oz	lb	lb	oz	lb oz
Brass*				4	7	93	3000	7			4	5	10
Brass*	31	2	26	4	2	93	3000	7			4	5	10
Brass*	25	2	0	3	11	93	3000	7			4	5	10
Brass*	11	2	3	3	1	93	3000	7			4	5	10

Brass – Bronze

Tables 4, 5 and 6 have been collated from the sources given in the reference list. Details regarding the charges of powder used may not be completely accurate, since these have been estimated from details given on a Gunners' Rule of the period. Proof charges for testing the gun were generally 30 per cent greater than the maximum service charge used (ie, maximum charge for maximum range). Shell charge refers to the actual charge contained within the shell. Scaling charge is assumed to be an increment used to vary the range.

FIRING THE MORTARS

Certain precautions were necessary to reduce the risk of fire or explosion aboard a bomb ship. First all lanterns, excluding those required in the magazine light rooms, were extinguished, as was the galley fire. Next the decks of the captain's cabin, the lower cabin flat and passageway to the magazine were wetted down. This practice was also carried out on the upper deck. Hide covers were rigged over the doors of the captain's cabin and the magazine, and these too were thoroughly soaked. Match tubs for the port fires, half filled with water or sand, were placed at each mortar.

All powder was measured out within the captain's cabin, with the door remaining shut at all times. Once the cartridges were filled, the amount of the charge was marked on each to prevent any possible confusion between the two mortars. If firing was to continue after nightfall all powder was measured out before dusk, and the cartridges stored until required. Likewise all shells were filled and fixed with their fuses before the bombardment took place.

During firing, calculations to correct range and trajectory were made. The gunner checked that all shells were of equal weight to prevent them falling short or overreaching their target. Replenishment of powder and shells was organised as required from the bomb tender, transfer being made by launches supplied from the accompanying fleet.

First the cartridge containing the charge was rammed down hard into the chamber; this was necessary as the black powder burnt slowly and required compression to attain the necessary power. Any excess space was filled with oakum wadding or old cordage. Next, a wooden wad was inserted, onto which the shell was lowered. Before the shell was loaded, the fuse cover was removed and the fuse cut to the required length. Extreme care was exercised when loading to ensure that the fuse was oriented uppermost and in line with the mortar's axis. To assist these requirements small wooden wedges were inserted around the windage.

By this period the precarious practice of double firing, where one of the RA matrosses lit the shell fuse while the other fired the mortar, was superseded by the single fire method. It had been found that the shell fuse could be lit instantaneously by the flash of the charge in the chamber, and this far safer practice was adopted.

MASTS AND YARDS

The *Granado* was a ketch-rigged vessel, having mainmast, mizzen mast and a bowsprit. The foremast was omitted to give greater room for the housing of the mortars. Both the main and the mizzen masts were made in three sections, a lower mast, topmast and topgallant mast. The bowsprit was also given an extension by the fitting of a jibboom, which carried the jibsail.

The absence of the foremast and its respective sail area made it necessary to increase the overall height of the mainmast to compensate for the reduction of sail area forward. This deficiency was also made up for by the rigging of additional, and larger sized, headsails. The ketch rig was never altogether satisfactory, as it was found to be very unmanageable in heavy weather; it was thus difficult to maintain the ship on station when sailing with a squadron. Later vessels were to be ship-rigged, which improved the sailing qualities, but inevitably reduced the arc of fire available to each mortar.

The masts were made from pine imported from either Riga or New England, each being made from a single tree; the lower mast was furnished with cheeks and bibs fitted separately. The heels of the lower masts were fashioned with a tenon which fitted into a mortice in the upper surface of the mast step. Each step was made from a baulk of oak, set astride the keelson and firmly bolted in position. The heel of the bowsprit was a tenon, which fitted into an angled step set between the forecastle and upper deck beams.

At the head of the lower masts a top was fitted. The tops were supported by crosstrees in the transverse plane and by tressletrees fore and aft. The heel of each topmast was set between the tressletrees and located with an iron fid, and further support was given to the topmast by the mast cap. The topgallant masts were retained in the same manner. The jibboom was also secured by means of a cap, through which it passed, fitted at the fore extremity of the bowsprit. The heel of the jibboom was set into a suitably shaped block, which formed a saddle over the upper surface of the bowsprit.

The yards, with the exception of the topgallants, crossjack and spritsail yards, were octagonal in cross-section at their centre portions, the remaining part of the yards being round. All the yards were fitted with two cleats at the centre, of a suitable length to retain the slings and parrel ropes. At the yardarms (outer extremities) cleats were also fitted on the fore and aft faces to act as stops for the various strops associated with the blocks and sails. The lower (or course) yards were made from two pieces of timber scarphed together, strengthened with battens nailed to the flats of the octagonal section.

Both masts were rigged with quadrilateral fore-and-aft sails; that fitted to the mizzen was termed the driver, while that fitted on the mainmast was known as the wingsail. Both these sails were rigged to a gaff yard at the head, and the driver also had a boom to spread the foot of the sail.

The tops fitted to the lower mast served a double function. First they spread the shrouds of their respective topmasts, and second, they provided a lookout position. This would have been particularly important when the mortars were being fired, so that corrections in trajectory and timing could be made. The tops were constructed of lightweight boards set up upon the crosstrees, with a rail fitted on the after side to give some degree of safety. The crosstrees fitted at the heads of the topmasts remained unplanked but nevertheless proved a suitable lookout post, if somewhat precarious.

RIGGING

In basic principles, the functions of the various ropes in the ketch rig differed very little to those of the more common ship rig. The rigging can be divided into two categories: standing rigging and running rigging. Standing rigging

TABLE 7: DIMENSIONS OF MASTS AND YARDS FOR THE GRANADO

Mast	Length yd	in	(Length) ft	in	Diameter in
Mainmast	24	0	72	0	24
Mizzen mast	20	0	60	0	16
Main topmast	14	0	42	0	12½
Mizzen topmast	8	24	26	0	7½
Main topgallant mast	7	0	21	0	7
Mizzen topgallant mast	4	12	13	0	4½
Bowsprit	16	24	50	0	20
Jibboom	10	6	30	6	8½
Yard					
Main yard	18	24	56	0	13
Mizzen crossjack	13	12	40	0	8
Main topsail yard	13	12	40	0	8
Mizzen topsail yard	7	26	23	2	4¾
Main topgallant yard	7	12	22	0	4¾
Mizzen topgallant yard*	4	20	13	8	3
Spritsail yard*	13	12	40	0	8
Wingsail gaff	6	0	18	0	5
Gaff	6	0	18	0	4
Boom	14	8	42	8	9

* If fitted – note that the mizzen topmast may have been made with a long polehead, the topgallant mast being completely omitted. The spritsail yard was not always carried.

TABLE 8: DIMENSIONS OF THE TRESTLETREES CROSSTREES AND MAST CAPS

TRESTLETREES	Length ft	in	Breadth ft	in	Depth in
Main	10	3		7	9¾
Mizzen	5	6		3½	4¾
Main topmast	4	3		3	4
Mizzen topmast	2	7		2	2½
CROSSTREES					
Main	13	3		7	4⅞
Mizzen	7	1		3½	2½
Main topmast	5	7		3	2
Mizzen topmast	3	6		2	1½
MAST CAPS					
Main	4	2	2	1	10
Mizzen	2	6	1	3	6
Main topmast	2	4	1	2	5½
Mizzen topmast	1	6		9	3¾
Bowsprit	3	7	1	9½	8½

both supported and braced the mast in both the fore-and-aft and transverse directions. These ropes were known as the backstays or forestays, and shrouds, respectively. Considerable attention was paid to the preparation, protection and setting up of this ropework, due to its importance in securing the masts. In all cases the ropework was well treated with tar to protect it from the elements and in various places it was further protected by being served, parcelled and wormed as necessary.

The forestay of the lower mainmast was set up with a suitably formed eye, which passed around the head of the mast. A stop known as a mouse was raised up on the rope to prevent the eye closing. This stay passed forward at an oblique angle to its securing point at the head of the ship. At this lower end a heart was seized to the loose end of the stay. A similar heart was seized to a collar, which passed around the inboard end of the bowsprit, and the two hearts were lashed together with a lanyard to bring the complete stay and collar to a state of tension. The forestay of the mizzen was set up in a similar manner, with the exception that the lower end was secured to the mainmast with two deadeyes; these again were lashed together with lanyards. The stays for the topmasts and topgallants were rigged in the same way as the mizzen lower stay, though in these cases a block was used instead of deadeyes. The fall of each stay passed to the deck via the associated block which was fastened to its respective masthead by a pendant.

The bowsprit was rigged with bobstays, which passed from the head of the bowsprit to the knee of the head. The lower end was formed into an eye which passed through a suitable hole in the head, and the upper end was secured to the bowsprit with deadeyes and lanyards.

Backstays were rigged to each masthead, and fastened with deadeyes to the channels at the ship's side. The shrouds of the lower masts were made up in pairs, each having an eye spliced into the bight; the eye passed over the head of the mast. The lower ends of the shrouds were secured to the channels with

deadeyes and lanyards, with the lower deadeyes fastened to the ship's side with chain plates. The shrouds of the topmasts and topgallant mast were rigged in the same manner, with their deadeyes fitted to the tops or crosstrees as suitable. Futtock shrouds were rigged between the lower shrouds and the tops, with their uppermost ends hooked to the topmast shroud chain plates. Once all of the shrouds were rigged they were 'rattled down' with their ratlines, which formed footholds for the seamen to ascend the mast.

The bowsprit shrouds were secured to a collar with deadeyes and lanyard fitted at the outer end of the sprit. The shrouds were led to the ship's side a little abaft the hawse holes, where they were secured with a hook and eyebolt.

The running rigging included all the cordage employed to manipulate the yards and sails, and all this ropework was left untarred to prevent snagging in the block sheaves. The rigging of the lower yards consisted of parrels, slings, jeers and lifts, their functions being to retain, raise and lower the yards. At the outer ends of the yards – the yardarms – braces were rigged to allow the yards be rotated about their axis on the mast. The topsail and topgallant sail yards were rigged in a similar fashion, with the exception that ties were used instead of jeers for raising the yards.

The rigging to the various sails amounted to a considerable quantity of cordage. For simplicity this can be divided into two categories: first there were ropes which were used for loosening and furling the sails, and second those which retained the sails taut in position when set.

In the first category, the rigging consisted of clewlines, buntlines and leechlines, each line pulling inward and upward from its respective point. The wingsail and gaffsail were rigged with brails, which served the same purpose. Additionally, most sails were rigged with leechlines and reef points, which were employed to shorten sail when required.

In the second category, each sail was furnished with tacks, sheets, bowlines and bridles, each retaining the sail in position.

The fore-and-aft staysails, including the jib sail, were in most cases set up on staysail stays, the upper end of which was seized to their respective stay. Each of these sails was hoisted by lanyards and lowered by downhaulers, and each was also rigged with sheets and tacks. The sheets consisted of two lines, whose use depended on the set of the sail necessary for tacking the ship.

TABLE 9: **RIGGING SIZES**

All sizes, in inches, refer to the circumference of the rope.

FORESTAYS

Mast	Stay	Stay collar	Lanyard	Worming
Main	12	8½	4	1
Mizzen	7½	6	2	¾
Main topmast	6	4½	2¼	–
Mizzen topmast	3¾	3	1½	–
Main topgallant mast	3	–	–	–
Mizzen topgallant mast	2	–	–	–

PREVENTER STAYS

Main	8¼	6	2¾	–
Mizzen	7	5¼	1¾	–
Main topmast	4½	3¼	1½	–
Mizzen topmast	3	2¼	1	–
Bobstay	4	4	1¾	–

SHROUDS AND BACKSTAYS

Mast	Shroud	Backstay	Lanyard	Futtock shrouds
Main lower	7¼	7¼	3½	5
Mizzen lower	6	6	3	3¾
Main topmast	5	5	2½	3
Mizzen topmast	3¾	3¾	2	2
Main topgallant mast	3	3	1*	–
Mizzen topgallant mast	2	2	¾*	–
Bowsprit	5	–	2	–

If fitted with deadeyes

MISCELLANEOUS STANDING RIGGING

Crowsfeet (main & mizzen)	1½
Bowsprit gammoning	5
Bowsprit horses	3
Mast wooldings (both masts)	2½
Cartharpins	2
Main stay tackle pendant	4½
Main stay tackle	4
Bowsprit shroud collar	4

THE RIGGING TO THE MAIN YARD AND MIZZEN CROSSJACK YARD

Item	Main yard	Mizzen crossjack
Jeer	7¾	–
Jeer falls	2¾	–
Slings	5	5
Truss pendant	–	4½
Truss falls	–	3¾
Parrel rope	4¾	4¾
Lifts	4	–
Lift span for the cap	4	–
Standing lifts	–	3
Standing lift lanyards	–	2
Footropes	3	3
Footrope lanyards	1¼	1¼
Stirrups	2½	2¼
Brace pendants	4	3
Braces	2½	2¼
Yard tackle pendant	4¾	4¾*
Yard tackle falls	2	2*
Yard tackle tricing line	1½	1½
Leechline, legs and falls	2½	–
Buntline, legs and falls	2⅛	–
Bowlines and bridles	3	–
Reef tackle pendants	3	–
Reef tackle falls	1¼	–

Item	Main yard	Mizzen crossjack
Reef tackle	1½	–
Sheets	4¾	–
Clue garnets	2 ¼	–
Tacks (widest part)	6	–
Earings	2	–

* If fitted

RIGGING TO THE MAIN AND MIZZEN TOPSAIL YARDS

Rigging	Main	Mizzen
Ties	4¾	3¾
Runner of the Tie	5	3¼
Halyard of the tie	3¼	3
Parrel rope	2¾	2½
Lifts	3⅛	2
Lift falls	3½	3
Footropes	3¼	2½
Footropes lanyards	1¼	1
Stirrups	2	2
Brace pendants	3¼	2½
Braces	2¼	1¾
Leechlines	2	1½
Buntlines	2¼	1½
Bowlines and bridles	2½	1½
Reef tackle	3	2
Reef tackle pendants	2¾	2¼
Reef tackle falls	1¾	1¼
Cluelines	2¾	2½
Sheets	5	3½
Earrings	1	1

RIGGING THE MAIN AND MIZZEN TOPGALLANT YARDS

Item	Main	Mizzen
Ties	2¾	2
Halyard of the tie	1½	1
Parrel rope	2	1¼
Lifts	2	1½
Footropes	2	1¾
Footrope lanyards	1	1
Stirrups	1½	1¼
Brace pendants	2	1
Braces	1½	1
Buntlines	1	¾
Bowlines and bridles	1½	1¼
Cluelines	1½	1¼
Sheets	3	2
Earrings	½	½

RIGGING TO THE SPRITSAIL YARD

Parrel rope	3½
Slings	4½
Halyard	4½
Lanyards	1⅛
Standing lifts	2¼
Standing lift lanyards	1⅛
Brace pendants	3½
Braces	3
Running lifts	2¼
Sheet pendants	3¾
Sheet strops	3
Cluelines	2¼
Footropes	2¾

TABLE 9: **RIGGING SIZES (continued)**

RIGGING TO THE SPRITSAIL YARD (continued)

Stirrups	2¾
Reef points	1⅛
Buntlines	2¼
Earrings	1⅛

RIGGING TO THE FORE-AND-AFT QUADRILATERAL SAILS

Item	Main wingsail	Mizzen gaffsail
Gaff parrel	5	5
Gaff topping lift	3¾	3¾
Vang pendants	4¼	4
Whips	2	2
Throat halyards	3¾	3¾
Boom topping lift	–	4½
Boom topping lift falls	–	2½
Boom sheets	–	3
Boom guy pendants	–	3
Guy falls	–	2¼
Earrings	1¾	1¾
Peak, middle and throat brails	2¼	2¼
Tacks	2½	2½
Sheets	3¾	3¾

RIGGING TO THE FORE STAYSAILS

Because the vessel was ketch fitted, this actually refers to those sails rigged from the mainmast to the bowsprit.

Item	Staysail	Topmast staysail	Jib
Staysail stay	–	2¾	2¾
Staysail, sail and/or stay halyard	3	2½	2¼
Staysail stay lanyard	–	1	½
Staysail stay tackle	–	2	1¾
Staysail stay tackle falls	–	2	1¾
Staysail sheet pendants	3	2¾	2¾
Staysail sheet whips	2¼	2	1¾
Tacks	2⅛	2	2
Downhauler	1½	1½	1¼
Outhauler	–	2¼	2
Outhauler tackle	–	2½	2¼
Netting, if rigged	1	1	¾

RIGGING TO THE FLYING JIBSAIL, IF CARRIED

Staysail halyard	2
Sheets and tacks	1½
Downhauler	1
Outhauler	1

RIGGING TO THE MIZZEN STAYSAILS

These sails were not always carried.

Rope	Mizzen staysail	Topmast staysail
Staysail halyard	2	1¼
Sheets	2	1¼
Tacks	1½	1⅛
Downhauler	1¼	1

MISCELLANEOUS ROPES

Catfalls	4
Backrope	2
Cat stopper	4
Shank painter tail	4¾
Fish pendant	6
Fish pendant tackle	3
Fish pendant fore guy	6
Fish pendant after guy	4
Anchor cable (4)	13
Additional anchor cable (1)	12
Kedge anchor cable	8¾
Messenger cable	9
Nippers, hook ropes and ring stoppers	1½
Bitt stoppers	6
Deck stoppers	10¾
Anchor bouy ropes	5¼
Anchor bouy slings	2¼
Gunport lid tackles	2
Breeching ropes	3
Muzzle lashings	2
Gun tackle	2

BOATS

Unfortunately, no information on the boats carried on the *Granado* is available. Existing evidence suggests that bomb vessels did not carry any boats. This suggestion is partly confirmed by the orders authorised to the bomb ship commander, which state that prior to action a request should be made to the admiral for the supply of two boats from the men-of-war. These were to attend both the bomb ship and its tender for conveying shells and stores. One would assume that such an order would be unnecessary if either the bomb ship or the tender had an available boat. In retrospect, however, it does seem improbable that neither vessel carried some form of boat, especially as boats were required for carrying dispatches, watering the ship, transferring stores and personnel and many other general duties.

By contrast, some sources do suggest that 10-gun sloops (equivalent in size to a bomb ship) were equipped with one 16ft long boat and one 24-ft pinnace. From this it could perhaps be construed that the *Granado* was probably furnished with a 16ft long boat when in service as a bomb ship, with the pinnace added when she served as a sloop. Whatever type and size of boat was carried, it would either have been towed astern or stowed above the after mortar housing. When required, the boat was either swung out or hoisted inboard from tackle suspended from the lower yards. These operations did present a number of difficulties, particularly on the smaller men-of-war; records show that complaints were common, and that some commanders preferred to have their boats towed astern.

CREW

When in service as a bomb ship, the *Granado* had a complement of sixty men. This total was divided into three groups: commissioned officers, warrant officers and seamen. Only two officers held the King's Commission, the commander and his lieutenant. In all probability the commander was a senior lieutenant by rank, his status of captain being in name only. The non-commissioned officers, who held the King's Warrant, were as follows: the master, surgeon, purser, boatswain, gunner, carpenter and the quartermaster. The remaining personnel comprised eleven able seamen and thirty ordinary seamen, all of whom were employed in sailing the ship and manning the

TABLE 10: LENGTH OF STROPS AND PENDANTS

Brace pendants	
Main yard	16ft 6in
Main topsail yard	12ft
Main topgallant yard	7ft
Crossjack	12ft
Mizzen topsail yard	7ft
Mizzen topgallant yard	4ft 3in
Spritsail yard	10ft
Main wingsail gaff vang pendants	9ft
Mizzen gaffsail vang pendants	9ft
Boom guy pendant	3ft
Spritsail sheet pendants	23ft
Spritsail sheet strops	7ft
Fish pendants	31ft

TABLE 11: SAIL SIZES

Sail	Cloths at		Boltropes at			
	Head	Foot	Head	Foot	Leech	Luff
Main course	24	24	1½in	3in	3in	–
Main topsail	16	24	1¼in	3in	3in	–
Main topgallant	8	16	1in	1¾in	1¾in	–
Mizzen topsail	9	16	1¼in	1½in	1½in	–
Mizzen topgallant	5	9½	¾in	1	1	–
Spritsail	18	18	¾in	1½in	1½in	–
Mizzen gaffsail (with boom)	7	20	1½in	2½in	2½in	–
Mizzen gaffsail (loose footed)	7	14	1¼in	2¼in	2¼in	–
Main wingsail	8	11	1¼in	2½in	2½in	–
Main lower stunsail	7	9	1in	1¼in	1¼in	–
Main topmast stunsail	6	8	1in	1¼in	1¼in	–
Jib	–	12½	–	1in	1in	1in
Main topmast staysail	–	12	–	1¼in	1¼in	1¼in
Main outer staysail	–	13	–	1¼in	1¼in	1¼in
Main staysail	–	11	–	1¼in	1¼in	1¼in
Mizzen staysail	–	10	–	1¼in	1¼in	1¼in
Mizzen topmast staysail	–	10	1in	1in	1in	1in

All the sail cloths are 2ft in width. Any fraction in the dimension of a sail is divided equally to each side. Rope sizes refer to circumference.

TABLE 12: ESTIMATED SAIL AREA OF THE GRANADO'S KETCH RIG

Sail	Area (sq ft)
Main course	1,608
Main topsail	1,440
Main topgallant	348
Mizzen topsail	60
Mizzen topgallant	140
Spritsail	468
Mizzen gaffsail (with boom)	818
Mizzen gaffsail (loose footed)	629
Main wingsail	694
Jib	682½
Main topmast staysail	589
Main outer staysail	450
Main staysail	330
Mizzen staysail	270
Mizzen topmast staysail	245
Main lower stunsail	544 (both 1,088)
Main topmast stunsail	462 (both 924)
Total:	11,323½

The sail referred to here as the main staysail was alternatively described as the fore course in the ketch rig.

defensive armament. In addition, there were two boatswain's mates, two carpenter's mates, an armourer, an officer's steward and the ship's cook.

Much to the detriment of the Navy, the overall responsibility for the mortars lay with a contingent of the Royal Artillery. This arrangement, which terminated in 1804, had been in force since the 1680s. The RA personnel lived aboard an accompanying tender ship and only embarked on the bomb vessel when required for action. The actual number of artillerymen allocated to one bomb ship is uncertain, however; by estimate, there were: three lieutenants, three sergeants, nine bombardiers, two or three gunner cadets, six gunners and fifteen matrosses. The latter often assisted in the defence of the ship.

Not only were the RA responsible for firing the mortars, they also organised the transportation of 'fixed' shells and other necessary stores from the support ship. Naval personnel were required to assist the artillerymen, the number allocated to each mortar being two warrant officers and eight to ten seamen. A second naval group, which included a warrant officer, carried out the duties of conveying the shells and powder cartridges from the magazines below decks. This work was controlled by a non-commissioned RA officer.

When the *Granado* served as a sloop, she carried a crew of 100 to 110 men. Apart from a general increase in the number of able and ordinary seamen, this included an additional three lieutenants, two midshipmen and a few extra warrant officers. This overall increase also permitted the Captain to have a greater number of stewards, since the rules stated that a captain was entitled to have four stewards for every 100 men in the crew.

APPENDIX 1: **THE DIMENSION AND SCANTLING LIST FOR THE** *GRANADO* **1742**

As noted above, the whereabouts of the contract for this ship is obscure; the following specifications have therefore been taken both from the original and from alternative contemporary draughts. Where necessary details were missing, the appropriate dimensions have been calculated from alternative sources, including draughts of similar-sized vessels and the Establishment lists.

		ft	in
Length of Keel for Tonnage		75	6
Length on the Range of the Deck from the Rabbet of the Stem to the Rabbet of the Post		91	1
Breadth, Extreme		26	2
Breadth of the After part of the Transom from out to outside of the Plank		17	8
Breadth at the Toptimber Line out to out	Afore	–	–
	Midships	23	2
	Abaft	12	8
Breadth of the Stern at the Fiferail		11	2
Height of the Toptimber line or Upper Edge of the Waist Rail above the bottom of the False Keel	Afore	22	0
	Midships	18	3
	Abaft	23	0
Depth in the Hold from the upper edge of the Limberstrake		11	3
Strake next the Limberboards – Limberstrake	Thick		6
	Broad (if can be had)	1	0
Burthen in Tons		266 92/94	
Draught of Water	Afore	8	9
	Abaft	9	1
Platform			
Abaft, height between Plank to Plank (at the middle of the Beams)		4	10
Afore, height between Plank to Plank (at the middle of the Beams)		5	10

After Accommodation (Cabin) Deck

		ft	in
Beams to round			3
Plank, thick			2
Height to the Upper Edge of the Quarter Deck at the middle of the Beam	Afore	5	3
	Abaft	6	3

Upper Deck

		ft	in
Beams to round			6
Plank, thick			2
Height to the Upper Edge of the Quarter Deck Beams at the middle of the Beams		3	9
Height to the Upper Edge of the Forecastle Beams at the middle of the Beams	Afore	4	9
	Abaft	4	3
Height to the Sweep Port Sills from the waterline midships		5	2
Height to the Gunport Sills from the waterline midships		5	2
Gunports	Deep	1	9
	Broad	2	0

Forecastle

		ft	in
Beams to round			4
Plank, thick			2
Length from the fore side of the Planking of the Bow		11	6

Quarter Deck

		ft	in
Beams to round			5
Plank, thick			2
Length, taken midships from the after part of the Counter Timbers		28	3
Length, from the fore side of the Tafferail at the height of the Fiferail to the fore side of the Figure of the Head in a line parallel to the Keel		103	2
Rounding of the Stern, at the Wing Transom			7
Rounding of the Stern at the Counter			8
Height of the Wing Transom above the upper edge of the Keel at the Post		13	9
Perpendicular Height above the upper edge of the Keel to the upper edge of the Plank at the middle line of the Upper Deck	Afore	14	5
	Abaft (Station 10)	13	7
Lower Height of the Breadth above the Upper edge of the Keel above the Dead Flat		9	10
Upper Height of the Breadth above the upper edge of the Keel at the Dead Flat		11	2
Height from the upper edge of the Keel to the Lower edge of the Counter Rail at the middle line		16	2
From the after side of the Wing Transom to the after part of the Counter			

		ft	in
Rail at the middle line		4	10

Parts of the Frame

		ft	in
Main Keel, of Elm or Beech, number of pieces not to exceed 4.			
Square in the Midships		1	0
Scarphs (laid with Tar and Hair), Thrice their Breadth or		3	4
Sided	Afore		10
	Abaft, at the Rabbet of the Post		8
Upper False Keel, thick			6
Lower False Keel, thick			2
Number of pieces for both, The same or One more than the Main Keel			
Stem, Main, Breadth or the Head athwartships		1	9
Fore and Aft at the Head			10
At the Foot, the same as the Main Keel			
Scarphs, not less than		3	0
No and size of Bolts in Each and to go through the False Stem; 6 of 7/8 ins Dia.			
False Stem (Apron) to overlaunch the scarphs of the Stem above and below	Thick		7
	Broad (if can be had)	1	6
Scarphs	long	1	0
Post, Main, Square at the upper end		1	4
Fore and aft on the Keel (False Post included, if fitted)		2	2
Abaft the Rabbet at the Wing Transom			6
Inner Post	Fore and aft on the Keel	1	0
	Fore and aft at the head		7½
Wing Transom, Sided			9
Moulded at the ends			8
Deck Transom, to lie close to the Cabin Deck for the Plank of the said Deck to bolt into the same Sided			6½
Moulded, as broad as conveniently may be for the better fastening of the Plank of the Deck			
Between the Wing Transom and Deck, so thick as to leave 2 inches between the Wing Transom and the Cabin Deck planking for the circulation of air			
Transoms, the Moulding of each to be 7 inches with spaces of no less than 2 inches between for the circulation of air.			
Rising Wood, a sufficient number of pieces afore and abaft.			
Abaft, (if a short piece of Keel) to overlaunch the Scarph at least 6 feet, if a long piece of Keel to drop short of the Scarph 7 feet.			
Depth in the Midships on the Keel		5	
Broad, in the Midships 3 inches on each side of the Keel (if can be had).			
Distance and Size of Bolts, Spaced every 20 inches, diameter being 1 inch			
Hawse Pieces. No each side, Three, and a piece between or Four if conveniently to be had and One Bollard timber.			
Hawse Holes, Diameter			8

Timbers

		ft	in
Room and Space		2	0
Floor and Futtock in the Bearing of the Ship to fill up the Rooms and Space Next the Flats Sided			11
Afore and Abaft			10½
At the Wrongheads at the Dead Flat, wrought in and out			9½
Afore and abaft, in and out			9
Every other bolted through the Keel with bolts of 1 inch diameter			
Heads to lie above the Bearing of the Floor		1	3
Foothooks; Lower sided in the Dead Flat next the Flats a small distance afore and abaft the Bearing of the Ship			10½
Afore and Abaft that stated above			10
In and out at the Heads in the Dead Flat			8
Foothooks, Second, Sided in the Midships			9½
Afore and Abaft, Sided			9
Foothooks, Upper, Sided in the Dead Flat			9
Afore and Abaft, Sided			8½
In and Out at their Heads			6½
Toptimbers, sided at the Heels and the Upper Foothook Heads			7
Side at the Heads			7
In and Out at the Gunnel or Top of the Sides			4
To be placed in wake of the Channels some on each side if can be had.			

In the Hold

		ft	in
Keelson, Square		1	0
Number of pieces if can be had; 4			
Length of the Scarphs to reach Three Floor Timbers and be bolted with bolts the same size of the Floor Timbers and Two Bolts in the ends of the Scarphs.			

Description		ft	in
Standard, Upon or under the Keelson abaft, the up and down arm to butt			
under the Lower Transom if can be had		4	3
The other Arm long		4	6
Sided at least			11
Limberstrake	Thick		6
	Broad	1	0
Thickstuff at the Floorheads, Middle Strake	Thick		5
	Broad, if can be had	1	2
Thickness of the Strakes above and below the Middle Strake			4
Number of Strakes above and below the Middle Strake; One.			
Thickstuff at the Lower Foothook Heads, Middle Strake	Thick		4
	Broad, if can be had	1	0
Strake above and below the Middle Strake, Thick			3
Footwaling (strake next to the Limberstrake),	Thick in the Midships		3
	Afore and Abaft		2½
Fore Platform Planking, Thick			2
After Platform Planking, Thick			1¾
Crotches, Number fitted; One			
Length of the Arm; as conveniently be had.			
Sided			9
No of Bolts of ⅞ inched Diameter; Six.			
Steps; Main, Sided, The Diameter of the Mast at the Partners,		2	3
or Deep on the Keelson		1	0
To be fastened with Six Bolts of 1 inch diameter.			
Mizzen, Sided		1	4
Deep on the Keelson; a sufficient Depth.			
Fastened with Six Bolts of ⅞ inches diameter.			
Breasthooks; Three Fitted below the Upper Deck Hook; Sided			10
Fastened with Seven Bolts of ⅞ inches diameter.			
Pillars, Upright under the Upper Deck Beams, Square			8
Well, Fore and Aft		2	0
Athwartships		7	6
Planking, Thick			1¾
Shot Locker, One Only fitted abaft the Well, Fore and Aft		2	0
Athwartships		7	6
Planking, Thick (integral with that of the Well)			1¾
Bulkheads, Length from the inside of the Rabbet on the Stern Post on the			
After Cabin Deck to the After side of the Magazine		8	0
Length from the inside of the Rabbet of the Stem Post on the Upper			
Deck to the After side of the After Bulkhead of the Fore Platform		18	6
Riders; Floor, Five below each Shell Room, Sided		1	1
Moulded on the Keelson		1	8
Length (athwartships)		13	6
Bolted with Fifteen Bolts of 1 inch diameter.			
Futtock, Scarphed to Floor Rider Heads; Sided		1	1
In and Out at the Heels		1	0
In and Out at the Heads			6
Bolted with Five Bolts of 1 inch diameter.			
Shell Room; Longitudinal Beams scored down onto Riders 3 inches.			
Length		12	3
Square		1	3
Pillars, Square			10
Longitudinal Beams, Upper	Length	12	3
	Square	1	3
Planking	Thick		2
	Broad	2	11
Mortar Pit; Beams, Six to each, Square		1	0
Clamps for Above to be wrought in One Strake Top and Butt.	Thick		6
	Broad	1	10
Pitt Deck Planking, lower layer (cyphered)	Thick		9
	Broad	1	2
Upper layer	Thick		5
	Broad		9
Longitudinal; Scored onto Mortar Pitt Beams 2 inches	Thick		11
	Deep	1	3
Trimmer Beam, wrought fore and aft;	Moulded		10
	Breadth	1	0
Standards, set upon the Mortar Pitt Beams, Sided			6
Up and Down Arm, length		1	8
Athwartships Arm length		1	9

Description		ft	in
Planking at the sides to be broad as can be had and thickness			6
Coamings and Head Ledges to be portable, thick			6
Filling Beams and Chocks to be wrought as convenient.			
Bolts used, for the Shell Room and Mortar Pitt timbers to 1, ⅞ and ¾ inches diameter.			
Bulkheads of the Cabins and Rooms of the Fore Platform to be Deal,			
Thick			1½
Bulkheads of the After Platform Cabins to be Deal, Thick			1½
Magazine Bulkheads to be Deal 1¾ inches thick.			
Deck hook; to be of the same scantling as the Breast Hooks.			
Length of the Arms, to be as convenient as can be had.			
Bolted with eight bolts ¾ inches in diameter.			
Fore Platform Beams	Sided		8
	Moulded		7
Carling to be wrought midships beneath the Firehearth,	Sided		9
	Moulded		8
Fore Bulkhead to be placed as convenient below the Bowsprit Step.			
After Platform Beams	Sided		8
	Moulded		6
Magazine Beams	Sided		7½
	Moulded		5½

After Cabin Deck

Description		ft	in
Length from the inside of the Rabbet of the Stern Post to the fore side of			
the foremost Cabin Deck Beam at the middle line		23	5
Bulkheads to be of Deal, Thick			1½
Beams, six in number to equally spaced or as convenient,	Sided		9
	Moulded		7
Clamps, to be wrought in a single Strake	Thick		6
	Broad		11
Knees, Sided	Lodging		6
	Hanging		7
Hanging Arm long (if can be had)		2	3
Lodging Arm to the Beam long		2	3
Hanging Knees to be Bolted with 6 Bolts of ¾ inches diameter.			
Carlings, Two tiers or where conveniently be placed	Broad		8½
	Deep		7
Ledges, to lie asunder not less than 9 inches, not more than 12	Broad		4
	Deep		3
Standards, to be fitted for the aftermost Beam in wake of the Hanging			
Knee, to be of the same scantling and bolted with 6 bolts ¾ inches in diameter.			
Transom Knees, to be fayed to the fore side of the Wing Transom and fastened with 6 bolts,			
⅞ inches in diameter.			
To be Sided, One inch less than the Moulding of the Transom.			
Length	fore and aft Arm	4	2
	Athwartships Arm	3	4
Waterway, Oak, Thick on the Chine, One inch greater than the Plank of the Deck.			
Ports, Two in number, the Sills to be at least Four Feet from the			
Waterline.	Broad	2	0
	Deep	2	0

Upper Deck

Description		ft	in
Clamps, to be wrought in Oak, Anchor Stock fashion with Hook and Butt.			
The lower edge to be two inches above the Mortar Pitt Beams for the circulation of air.			
Thick at the Upper Edge			5
Thick at the Lower Edge			4
Beams, Sided		1	0
	Moulded		11
To lie where they can conveniently be placed.			
Knees, Double at each end, Hanging and Lodging, Sided			7
The Up and Down Arm to reach the Mortar Pitt Beam Clamps		3	0
Athwartships Arm long		2	9
To be fastened with Seven Bolts of ¾ inches diameter.			
Carlings, Two tiers on each side except in wake of Hatchways and Masts	Broad		6½
	Deep		5
Those fitted as Coamings to be Oak, let down into the Beams 1 inch.			
Coamings to lie above the Deck			9
Broad with the Rabbet			6
Ledges; To lie asunder, no less than 9 inches and no more than 12 inches.	Broad		4½
	Deep		3½
Waterway; Thick on the Chine; One inch more than the Flat of the Deck.			
Partners, for the Mainmast, to be of Oak	Thick	1	3
	Deep	1	4
To lie above the Flat of the Deck			4
For the Mizzen Mast, to be of Oak	Thick	1	0
	Deep		6

Bowsprit Step, to be made from two baulks of Oak, overall Athwartships		3	0
	Thick		6
Plank, on the Flat; Three Strakes next the Waterways and all the Forepart			
of the Deck to be of English Oak	Thick		2
Two (Binding) Strakes next the Coamings to be One Inch thicker than the rest of the Deck and			
to be let down One Inch on the Beams and tailed and hooked into the Deckhook. To be Bolted			
with Two small bolts in each Beam and One Treenail in each Ledge. The size of the Bolts to be			
½ inch and to be in length One Inch longer than Twice the Thickness of the Plank.			
All the rest of the Plank to be of Prussia Deal bolted with One Bolt in			
each Beam and One Treenail in each Ledge, to be Thick			2
Carrick Bitts, to be of Oak; The foremost edge to be Abaft the Rabbet of the Stem		11	0
Distance between them Athwartships		7	4
The Heads to be Broad Athwartships			7½
Fore and Aft		1	9
The Heads to be above the Deck at the middle line		5	2
The Pins to taper from the lower edge of the Deck Beams to their Heels,			
fore and aft		1	2
Hatches, Main	Fore and aft	4	10
	Athwartships	4	10
	Fore and aft	2	10
	Athwartships	4	10
Manger, Plank Thick			2
Scuppers, number on each side, 2; Each of 4 inches diameter.			
Scuppers at the Ship's Side, number; 4 each side of 4 inches diameter.			
Spirketting, to be wrought in Two Strakes, Top and Butt on each side to			
the level of the Gun Port sills.	Thickness at the		
	uppermost edge		
	Thickness at the lowermost edge	4	
			4½
Stringer in the Waist, made lateral with the Planksheer.			
Bitts, Main Topsail Sheet and Jeer, Square			8
Height above the Deck		3	8
To be fashioned with a Standard at their Heels			
Sheet and Jeer Crosspieces	Fore and Aft		7½
	Deep		6
	Scored into the Bitts		1¾
Bolts, Ring and Eye for the Ports, Four in number each Port, diameter			¾
Diameter of the Rings in the Clear			4
On the flat of the Deck for the Guns, Size			¾
Eye for lashing the Blocks on each side of the Mainmast, Size			¾
Ditto, for the Toptackles, Diameter			1¼
Span Shackle (the corners of the Shackle to be round), Size			1¼
Number fitted, Two.			

Quarter Deck

Clamps, Upper Edge	Thick		3¾
Lower Edge	Thick		3
	Broad (if can be had)		9
Beams, to have a Small Strap of Iron round the Timber to every Second			
and Third Beam in Wake of the Cabins	Sided		7
	Moulded		5
To lie asunder from 2 feet to 2 feet 2 inches where they can be conveniently placed.			
To be bolted into the Clamps at their ends with Bolts of ¾ inches diameter.			
Knees Hanging, Sided (if fitted)			5
(These were not generally fitted, however if they were the Up and Down Arm would have been			
worked down to Lintels of the Ports and the athwartships Arm being approximately 2 feet			
in length. The knees would have been fastened with Bolt of ⅝ inches diameter.)			
Two Transom knees to be fitted to the foreside of the Deck Transom,			
to be Sided			5
The Athwartships Arm long		2	10
To be fastened with 5 Bolts of ¾ inches diameter.			
Waterways, Thick on the Chine; One inch thicker than the Plank of the Deck.			
Quickwork, berthed up with Deal, Thick			1½
Rudder Head Housing, Deal Boards, Thick			1

Forecastle

Clamps; Upper edge	Thick		3½
Lower Edge	Thick		3
	Broad (if can be had)		9
Beams, To be fitted as convenient	Sided		7
	Moulded		5
Knees; Two to be fitted to the Aftermost Beam	Sided		5
The Up and Down Arm long, To reach the Spirketting			

The Athwartships Arm long		2	10
Fastened with Six Bolts ⅝ inches in diameter.			
Partners for the Bowsprit, Sided			7
Moulded			4½
Waterways, Thick on the Chine, One inch thicker than the Plank of the Deck.			
Quickwork, Berthed up with Deal, Thick			1½
Catheads, Square			10

Without Board

Wales, Main and Stuff Between to be an equal Thickness, to be wrought			
with Hook and Butt. Deep from the Upper to Lower Edge		2	6
Planks to be Thick			4
One Strake above them, Thick			3
Strake below the Wales (Diminishing Strakes), Two Strakes fitted.			
Thickness at the Upper Edge of the Upper Strake			3
Thickness at the Lower Edge of the Lower Strake			2½
The Rest of the Plank under the Thickstuff to be wrought full to the Floors with Oak and			
the lower Four Strakes with Elm, Thick			2
Deal in the Waist at the Top of the Side, Thick			2
Channels; Main, Length of the Fore Part		6	3
Length of the After Part		9	0
Breadth at the Foremast end to be sufficient to Carry the Shrouds		1	8
clear of the Gunnell			
Thickness, at the Inner Edge			4
at the Outer Edge			2½
Mizzen, Length		7	9
Breadth		1	3
Thickness, at the Inner Edge			3
at the Outer Edge			2½
Main Topgallant Backstay Stool	Long	1	6
	Breadth	1	1
Thickness, to be the same as the Mizzen Channel.			
All channels to be fastened with Bolts of ¾ diameter.			
Chain Plates, Main, Broad			3
Thick in the Middle			1
Thick at the Edges			⅝
Size of the Bolts			1¼
Mizzen, Broad			2½
Thick in the Middle			⅞
Thick at the Edges			½
Size of the Bolts			1⅛
Plates, Ring and Backstay for the Main Chains to have the same Breadth and Thickness and the			
same size Bolts as the Main Chain.			
Bindings, for the Main Deadeyes, Size			1¼
for the Mizzen Deadeyes, Size			1⅛
Deadeyes for the Main Channels, number fitted including One Spare, Seven.	Diameter		11
	Thickness		6¼
For the Mizzen Channels, number fitted, Four.	Diameter		9
	Thickness		5
For the Main Topmast Backstays, Two of Nine Inches diameter.			
Main Topgallant Backstay, One of Seven Inches diameter			
Mizzen Topmast Backstay, One of Seven Inches diameter.			
Mizzen Topgallant Backstay, One of Five Inches diameter.			
Rother [Rudder] Head, Athwartships (if can be had)		1	3
Fore and Aft (if can conveniently be had)		1	1
At the Lower End, Fore and Aft, One Tenth of the Ships Extreme Breadth			
or as convenient		4	0
Braces and Pintles, Number of Pair, 5.			
Upper Afore and Rabbet of the Post, Long		2	3
Lower Afore the Back of the Post, Long		5	0
To be Hung Flemish Fashion and secured with Chocks above the waterline to prevent			
its unhanging.			
Pintles, Diameter			2½
Length of the Upper Pintles			9
Length of the Lower Pintle only to be			11
Braces and Straps for the Pintles, Broad			4
Thick in the Shoulder at the Return			1½
To have an Iron Strap on the Back and on each Corner and Eye well Clenched on the side of			
the Strap of Sufficient Bigness to receive an Oval Ring			
Head; The Knee to be as Thick as the Stem			
Size of the Upper Two Bolts to be in diameter			1⅜
Size of the Upper Two Bolts in the Stem			1⅜

Cheeks, Sided, if can be had	Lower	6	The Fife Rail, (Drift rail)	Broad 7 / Thick 3
	Upper	5	Drift to be struck with an Astrical within and without.	

Cheeks, Sided, if can be had — Lower 6, Upper 5
Length of the Arm next the Side (if can be had), (approximately) — 5 9
To be fastened with Bolts the same size as the Upper Deck knees.
Head Timber, Sided — 6 to 4
Length from the Fore side of the Stem to the Fore part of the Knee of the Head — 4 6
Standard in the Head, Sided, (Bolted as the Upper Deck Knees) — 8
Upper Rails at the after end, Fore and Aft — 7½
Athwartships — 5½
Chesstrees, Sided at the Gunwale — 4½
Fenders, Sided at the Gunwale — 3½
Asunder, no less than — 1 3
Lining of the Anchors, to be of Elm, Thick — 2
Rails on the Side, The Sheer (also acts as the Planksheer) — Broad 8 / Thick 7

The Fife Rail, (Drift rail) — Broad 7 / Thick 3
Drift to be struck with an Astrical within and without.
Shankpainter, Long (estimated) — 9 6
Size of the Links — ¾
Port Hinges, – not stated. (likewise the Bucklers – Sweep Port hinges).
Bolts for the Butt ends under water where they are necessary to be placed in the
Timber next the Butt and to be Clenched within side, Size, (diameter) — ¾
Eye, for the Standing part of the Main Sheets, Size — 1¼
for the Mizzen Sheet, Main Brace, Main Topsail Halliard, Bowsprit Shrouds, and in
Wake of the Chain Plates, Size — 1
for the Mizzen Topsail Halliard and Mizzen Truss, Size — ¾
Lining of the Hawse, between the Holes, Thick — 4½
Bolt holes to be Bored through, Size — ¾

APPENDIX 2: PROGRESS BOOK – GRANADO

Granado Built by Admiralty Order 14th September, 1741

At what Port	Arrived	Docked Grounded or Careend	Where Sheathed	Graved	Launched	Sailed	Nature of the repair	Charge £.s.d. of Hull, Masts & Yards	Rigging & Stores	Total	Observations
Ipswich											
John Barnard	Began	18 Nov 1741	–	June 1742	22 Jun 1742	23 Jun 1742	Built	2870. 5. 0	–	–	
Harwich	25 Jun 1742	–	–	–	–	Aug 1742	Fitted as a Sloop	294.10. 3	1150. 3. 8	1444.13.11	
Sheerness	5 Sep 1742	9 Sep 1742	–	Sep 1742	10 Sep 1742	26 Sep 1742	Req'd. D⁰	80.10. 1	36.13. 4	117.11. 5	(a) Admty Order 4 July 1742 to be fitted as a Sloop
Portsmouth	29 Nov 1742	4 Dec 1742	–	Dec 1742	6 Dec 1742	23 Dec 1742	Refitted	70. 0.11	82.17. 4	152.18. 3	
Plymouth	7 May 1743	10 May 1743	–	May 1743	11 May 1743	31 May 1743	D⁰	61.11. 7	374. 7. 3	435.18.10	
Sheerness	17 Nov 1743	29 Nov 1743	–	Dec 1743	2 Dec 1743	25 Dec 1743	D⁰	167. 7. 7	712. 8. 5	879.16. 0	
Portsmouth	25 May 1744	27 May 1744	–	May 1744	29 May 1744	5 Jun 1744	D⁰				
Portsmouth	6 Oct 1744	9 Oct 1744	–	Oct 1744	12 Oct 1744	26 Oct 1744	D⁰	172. 2. 1	655. 8. 5	827.10. 6	
Woolwich	31 May 1745	3 Jun 1745	–	G.& Tall*	18 Jun 1745	1 Jul 1745	D⁰	–	–	–	(b) Admty Order 20 June 1745 to have 110 men & 2 more guns
Woolwich	8 Aug 1745	10 Aug 1745	–		20 Aug 1745	1 Sep 1745	D⁰	866. 0. 6	619. 7. 3	1485. 7. 9	(c) Admty Order 30 July 1745 to fit her as a Bomb.
Woolwich	–	20 Aug 1745	–	G.& Tall*	27 Aug 1745	1 Sep 1745	D⁰	–	–	–	(d) Admty Order 17th Aug 1745 to fit her as a Sloop
Sheerness	29 Jan 1746	8 Jul 1746	–	Jul 1746	9 Jul 1746	16 Jul 1746	D⁰	–	–	–	
Sheerness	30 Oct 1746	17 Nov 1746	–	Nov 1746	24 Nov 1746	3 Dec 1746	D⁰	292. 6. 4	1146. 5. 8	1438.12. 0	
Sheerness	8 Mar 1747	14 Mar 1747	–	Mar 1747	20 Mar 1747	25 Mar 1747	D⁰				
Sheerness	19 Jun 1747	29 Jun 1747	–	Jun 1747	4 Jul 1747	21 Jul 1747	D⁰	325.16. 9	354. 8. 5	680. 5. 2	(e) Surveyed on Wed 10th Dec 1748 and found to want small repair Est. for the Hull £500 & 6 weeks. Repaired & completed 16th Aug. 1749
Sheerness	10 Mar 1748	30 Mar 1748	–	Apr 1748	6 Apr 1748	22 Apr 1748	D⁰	203.18. 6	639. 4. 9	843. 3. 3	
Woolwich	12 Sep 1748	7 Jul 1749	–	Jul 1749	21 Jul 1749	–	Small repair	213.16. 5	1.15. 8	215.12. 1	(f) Admty Order 17th Feb 1755 forthwith to put her in condition for service
Woolwich	–	26 Feb 1755	–	Mar 1755	15 Mar 1755	14 Jun 1755	Fitted	1102.18. 7	1228. 4. 1	2331. 2. 0	(g) Admty Order 26 Jul 1756 to fit her at Woolwich for Channel Service as a Bomb vessel to carry 60 men
Sheerness	4 Jul 1755	5 Jul 1755	–	Jul 1755	6 Jul 1755	7 Jul 1755	Refitted	96.10. 0	143.10. 0	240. 8. 0	
Portsmouth	13 Sep 1755	10 Sep 1755	–	Sep 1755	19 Sep 1755	1 Oct 1755	D⁰	108.16.11	49.11. 4	168. 8. 3	
Sheerness	19 Nov 1755	23 Nov 1755	–	Nov 1755	24 Nov 1755	13 Dec 1755	D⁰				(h) Admty Order 26th Apr 1756 to fit her as a Bomb Vessel
Sheerness	10 Feb 1756	17 Feb 1756	–	Feb 1756	24 Feb 1756	3 Mar 1756	D⁰	–	–	–	
Sheerness	16 May 1756	23 May 1756	–	May 1756	23 May 1756	6 Jun 1756	D⁰ }				
Sheerness	26 Jun 1756	27 Jun 1756	–	Jun 1756	20 Jun 1756	30 Jun 1756	D⁰	279. 3. 2	490. 0. 6	769. 3. 8	
Woolwich	8 Aug 1756	12 Aug 1756	–	Sep 1756	9 Sep 1756	25 Sep 1756	D⁰	594. 5. 5	220. 9. 6	814.14.11	
Sheerness	1 Jan 1757	6 Jan 1757	–	Jan 1757	8 Jan 1757	23 Jan 1757	D⁰	118.12. 6	104.15.10	303. 8. 4	
Woolwich	27 Feb 1757	5 Mar 1757	–	Mar 1757	17 Mar 1757	29 Mar 1757	Fitted	606. 2. 5	188. 0. 1	794. 2. 6	
Portsmouth	11 Dec 1757	20 Feb 1758	–	Mar 1758	1 Mar 1758	11 Mar 1758	Refitted	–	–	–	

Port								£ s d	£ s d	£ s d	Notes
Portsmouth	9 Apr 1758	12 May 1758	–	May 1758	13 May 1758	17 May 1758	Fitted }	549. 2.11	1412. 9. 9	1961.12. 8	
Portsmouth	21 Sep 1758	30 Sep 1758	Oct 1758	Oct 1758	4 Oct 1758	10 Oct 1758	Do }				
Portsmouth	7 Oct 1759		Oct 1759	–	–	–		–	–	–	
Portsmouth	7 Oct 1759	7 Apr 1760	–	Apr 1760	9 Apr 1760	27 Apr 1760	Refitted as }	335. 9. 4	817. 6. 7	1152.15.11	{ (j) Admty Order 20th Mar 1760 to fit her for a Sloop
Portsmouth	18 Sep 1760	6 Oct 1760	Replaced	Oct 1760	9 Oct 1760	10 Oct 1760	a sloop }				
Sheerness	17 Dec 1760	20 Dec 1760	–	Dec 1760	30 Dec 1760	9 Jan 1761	Do	203.10. 5	256.10. 6	460. 8.11	
Portsmouth	30 Mar 1761	15 Apr 1761	–	Apr 1761	16 Apr 1761	24 Apr 1761	Do	238.17. 4	431. 2.11	670. 0. 3	
Portsmouth	28 Jul 1761	3 Aug 1761	–	Aug 1761	4 Aug 1761	1 Sep 1761	Fitted for a Bomb				
Woolwich	16 Jun 1763	At Portsmouth	1763	–	–	–		8. 7. 4	130.18. 5	139. 5. 9	(k) Surveyed afloat 6th July, 1763 & found to want large repair. Est. for the Hull £1356 and 9 months; 7 July proposed to be sold with stores. (l) Admty Order 20th July 1763 to sell her with stores.

Sold 30th August 1763 for £575.

Graved and Tallowed

Reference Adm 180/3, entries 477 and 480 (PRO)

APPENDIX 4: **RECORDS OF WEIGHTS AND STORES ON BOMB VESSELS**

BALLAST AND WEIGHTS OF BOMB VESSELS, 1759

Deptford Yard. 24th June, 1759

Pursuant to your instructions I send you undermentioned an account to the quantity of Ballast, weight of Mortars and draughts of water of the two bombs at this Port, viz:—

Carcass

Ballast	Iron	20 tons			
	Shingle	0			
Draught without Mortar	Afore	9ft 8in			
	Abaft	11ft 1in			
		tons	**cwt**	**qtr**	**lb**
Mortar weight	13 inch	4	7	0	10
	10 inch	1	12	2	20
		5	19	3	2
Mortars aboard – Draught	Afore	10 ft 0in			
	Abaft	11ft 2½in			

Mortar

Ballast	Iron	20 tons			
	Shingle	10 tons			
Draught without Mortars	Afore	9ft 11in			
	Abaft	11ft 2in			
		tons	**cwt**	**qtr**	**lb**
Mortar weight	13 inch	4	8	0	6
	10 inch	1	14	8	26
		6	4	3	4
Draught with Mortar	Afore	10ft 3in			
	Abaft	11ft 3in			

I am Sir
Your Most Honble Servant
Adam Hayes

Hon. Thos. Slade, Esq.

Note that the Carcass referred to here was ship-rigged, and not of the 1740 bomb vessel type; the Mortar on the other hand was one of the last ketch-rigged bombs built, by Wells (Thames).

Reference ADM 95/66 Letter 16

WEIGHT OF THE MORTARS AND BOMB BEDS – BOMB VESSEL FURNACE, 1757

Woolwich. 10th March, 1757

Furnace Bomb, weight of Mortars and Bomb Beds
Aggreable to your request written on the 6th, the Furnace Bomb, Undermentioned is the weight of her Mortars and Bomb Beds which brought her (draught) down 3 inches.

	tons	cwt	qtrs	lbs
Mortar of 13 inches	4	1	1	18
Bed for Ditto	2	10	1	3
Mortar of 10 inches	1	18	2	14
Bed for Ditto	1	12	3	7
Total	10	3	0	14

Signed

Honorable Thos. Slade Esq.

Reference Adm 95/65 (PRO)

INVENTORY OF SMALL ARMS TO BE CARRIED ON A SLOOP

Muskets with Slings and Cartridge Boxes	80
Pistols in pairs with Hooks	30
Swords with Belts and Frogs for Bayonets	80
Bayonets	80
Pole Axes, well steeled	20
Hand Grenades	80
Iron Crowes	10
Drum	1

Although the Granado was rated as a bomb vessel, much of her career was spent carrying out the duties of a Sloop, and at various periods she was actually converted, and listed as a Sloop.
Reference Adm 95/65 (PRO)

WEIGHT OF STORES ETC FOR THE THUNDER AS COMMISSIONED, 1759

A calculation of the weight of the Masts and Yards, ordnance, naval and victualling stores & Etc., aboard His Majesty's Bomb the 'Thunder' at her sailing from Black Stakes the 27th July, 1959.

Provisions

	Puncheon	Hogshead	Half Hogshead	Weight tons	cwt	qtr	lb
Water in the Ground Tire [Tier]	7	50	22	17	11	2	10
Beer in the Second Tire [Tier]	35	–	–	11	13	0	20
All Species of dry and wet provisions	–	–	–	3	9	0	24
Coals, Wood and Candles	–	–	–	3	12	0	0
To what time the above Provisions were Complete for the Complement of	Three months						
Men (60)				36	5	3	26
Bricks, Tyles, Stone, Mortar, Ironwork & Lead				4	2	1	0
Iron Ballast				20	2	0	0
Shingle Ballast				30	0	0	0
Masts & Yards Complete				21	15	0	8

Cordage

		tons	cwt	qtr	lb
Rigging & Fitting	Blocks, Dead eyes, Thimbles & Hooks	9	10	2	14
		4	2	1	7
the same	Other Stores expend about the Rigging	0	5	3	0
		4	8	0	7

Cables and Other Cordage

		tons	cwt	qtr	lb
		11	18	3	5
Boatswain's Sea	Anchors	3	3	3	10
Stores for	Sails	2	6	1	19
8 months	Boats	1	10	0	0
	All other Sea Stores	4	10	2	14
Carpenters Sea Stores for 8 months		9	4	3	0

Ordnance

	No	Pound	tons	cwt	qtr	lb
Gun Upper Deck	8	6	6	14	2	23
Gun Carriages	8	–	1	12	0	0
Mortar of 13 inches	1	–	4	7	1	20
10 inches	1	–	1	16	2	16
Beds to the Mortars	2	–	3	6	0	0
Round Shot of 6 Pound & ½ Pound	–	–	2	7	1	22
Grape Shot of 6 Pound & ½ Pound	–	–	0	6	0	20
Powder in half Barrels	44	–	1	2	0	0
All other Stores for the Gunner in Gross	–	–	2	6	0	0
Seamen with their chests and bedding	–	–	5	17	2	0
Total*			188	14	1	8

Draught of Water

Afore 12.4
Abaft 12.5

Height of the upper side of the lower cells of the upper Deck Ports from the water.

Afore 6.1
Midships 4.8
Abaft 5.7

Chatham Yard. 2nd August, 1759.

* *Final total calculated and added by the author.*

Reference ADM 95/66 Letter 17

Sources

Blackmore, H L *The Armouries of the Tower of London* HMSO, 1976
Bruce, G *Harbottle Dictionary of Battles* Granada
Corbett, Sir Julian S *England and the Seven Years War 1752–63* 2nd Edition
  Vols I & II
Eggenberger, D *A Dictionary of Battle from 1479 BC* Allan & Unwin, 1967
Goodwin, P *The Construction and Fitting of the Sailing Men of War 1650–1850*
  Conway Maritime Press, 1987
  The Anatomy of the 20-Gun Ship Blandford Conway Maritime Press, 1988
Hogg, I & Batchelor, J *Naval Gun* Blandford Press, 1978
Hough, R *Fighting Ships* Michael Joseph, 1969
Howard, E *Genoa – History and Art of an Old Seaport* Sayep SpA Genova, 1978
Lavery, B *The Arming and Fitting of English Ships of War 1600–1815* Conway
  Maritime Press, 1987
Lees, J *The Masting and Rigging of English Ships of War 1625–1860* Conway
  Maritime Press, 1979
May, Cdr W E *Boats of Men of War* NMM
Munday, J *Naval Cannon* Shire Publications
Padfield, P *Guns at Sea* Hugh Evelyn, 1973
Ranft B McL *The Vernon Papers* Navy Records Society, vol XCIX
Sanderson, M *Sea Battles* David and Charles, 1975
Upham, N E *Anchors* Shire Publications
Wilkinson-Latham, R *British Artillery on Land and Sea 1790–1820* David &
  Charles, 1973

Progress Books 1 & 2

Dimension Book B

Articles from Model Shipwright (Conway Maritime Press)
'Bomb Vessels – Their Development and Use', by David Wray, *MS* 25, 26, 27
'Granado', by Bob Lightley, *MS* 16, 17, 18, 19
'Sea Mortars', by Dr Milton Roth, *MS* 40
'An English Ketch-Rigged Sloop', by W H Shoulder, *MS* 3, 4, 5, 6, 7, 8
'Fittings for Wooden Warships' Part 2, by Robert Gardiner, *MS* 19

PRO References

Captain's Log *Granado*

Adm 51/412	25/4/1742 to 3/10/1744
	13/10/1744 to 24/9/1748
Adm 51/4203	25/4/1755 to 30/4/1756
Adm 51/413	1/5/1756 to 14/10/1757
	20/1/1758 to 17/2/1760
	23/2/1760 to 23/2/1761
	27/3/1762 to 1/7/1762
Adm 51/397	2/7/1762 to 23/6/1763

Master's Log *Granado*

Adm 52/607	13/8/1742 to 31/7/1743
	9/9/1744 to 24/6/1745
	20/11/1745 to 15/4/1748
Adm 52/875	23/2/1756 to 2/9/1757
	8/9/1757 to 22/8/1759
Adm 52/874	24/8/1759 to 16/9/1760
	12/10/1760 to 22/6/1763

Ship's Muster Books *Granado*

Adm 36/1308	1742–43
Adm 36/1309	1743–44
Adm 36/1310	1744
Adm 36/1311	1745
Adm 36/1312	1745–46
Adm 36/1313	1746–47
Adm 36/1314	1747–48
Adm 36/1315	1742–46
Adm 36/1316	1746–48
Adm 36/5688	1755–56
Adm 36/5689	1756–58
Adm 36/5690	1758–62
Adm 36/5691	1762–63

Progress Books	Adm 180/3
Armament	Adm 180
Letter Books	Adm 106
In letters	Adm 1
Out letters	Adm 2
Sailing qualities	Adm 95/23
	Adm 95/24
	Adm 95/25
	Adm 95/26
	Adm 95/27
Other sources	Adm 95/12
	Adm 95/17
	Adm 95/65
	Adm 95/66

Draughts used

Granado	(1742) Profile, half breadth & body plan, No 4316 Box 61
Blast	(1759) Profile, No 4308 Box 61
Blast	(1759) Deck arrangements & sections, No 4309 Box 61
Blast	(1740) Profile, half breadth & body plan, No 4313 Box 61
Basilisk	(1740) Profile, half breadth and deck plans, Danish Archives, Rigsarkivet, Copenhagen

The Photographs

2. Overall view of the *Granado*, illustrating deck layout, quarterdeck bulkhead, disposition of beams, carlings and ledges and external fittings. *NMM*

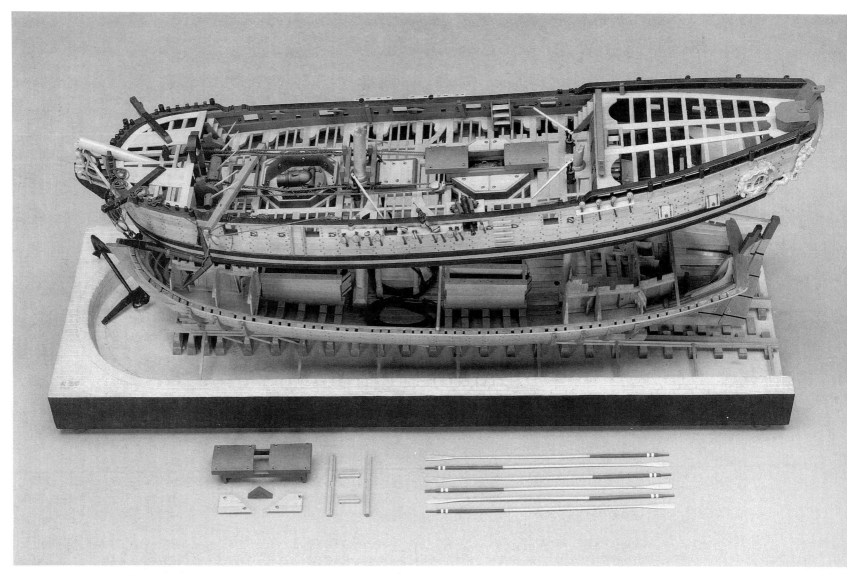

3. A top view of the hull, illustrating the layout of the deck, with various housing accessories and sweeps in the foreground.
NMM

4. Port bow view of the *Granado*, illustrating the head timbers and figure, anchor and accessories including its buoy. *NMM*

5. Port broadside view, showing external features and illustrating the modelmaker's ingenuity in showing off the interior of the hull. *NMM*

6. Starboard side view of the interior, showing the breadroom, magazine, filling room and light box; also shown are the after platform, cabins and the after shell room. *NMM*

7. Port side view of the interior, showing the arrangement of the fore platform, forward shell room, mainmast step and cable tier. The galley firehearth can just be seen at top left. *NMM*

8. The fore part of the upper deck, showing the forecastle, forward mortar housing, windlass and cable arrangements and the fish davit. *NMM*

9. Overall view of the after part of the upper deck, illustrating the after mortar housing partially disassembled, the two sets of pumps, swivel gun and 4-pounder cannon. *NMM*

10. Detail of the after 10in mortar, showing the various fittings including the chock. The ringbolts fitted to the mortar pit housing were employed for tackle to rotate the mortar bed. *NMM*

11. Stern view, showing the cabin lights, tafferal adornment and quarter figures. The transoms, fashion piece and framing of the stern are also clearly shown. *NMM*

12. View of the starboard quarter, illustrating the carved work of the stern and quarter badge. *NMM*

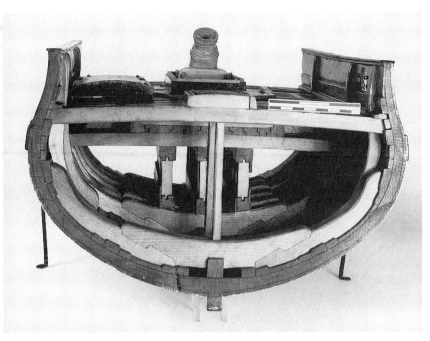

13. Midship section of a Bomb Vessel. This particular model represents a ship-rigged bomb of the latter half of the eighteenth century; the photograph clearly illustrates the construction, showing the floor and futtock riders, shell room beams and pillars and mortar pit deck and housing. The housing canopy (removed) can be seen on the left side of the upper deck. Of particular interest are the breast riders (a later adoption) and the rabbeted planks of the mortar pit deck. *Courtesy of the Pitt Rivers Museum*

14. (Above right) Detail of the shell room on the same model, illustrating the floor riders, longitudinal beams, support pillars and bulkhead planking (one strake omitted for clarity). The head and heel tenons for the pillars, however, do not conform to general construction practice. The shell stowage racks between the pillars have been omitted. *Courtesy of the Pitt Rivers Museum*

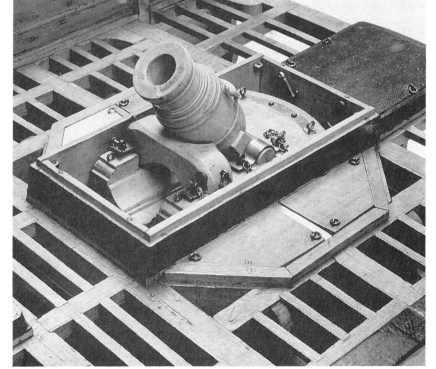

15. Detail of a 13in mortar and bed. Unlike that of the *Granado*, with its iron support, this mortar is furnished with a timber support chock fixing the mortar elevation at 45 degrees. This chock is maintained in position by right angled iron keep plates and retaining pins. *Courtesy of the Pitt Rivers Museum*

16. A contemporary model of a bomb vessel of circa 1695. Note the mortars of the earlier design, cast integral with a bedplate. The model also clearly illustrates the lute stern, a common feature of the earlier types. This model has since been lost. *Science Museum*

The Drawings

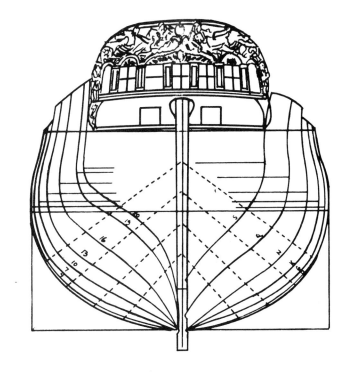

Grand Bomb Built by Mr Jno Barnard
at Ipswich and Launch'd 22 June 1742
Length on the Range of the Deck ---- 91·1 ins
Breadth Extream ------------ 26·7 ----
Berthen in Tuns ------- 266:93/94
Depth in Hold ------------ 11·3
Draught of water when launch'd Bilways Off ----- { afore 8·9
And no anchors at ye Bows or furnaces { abaft 9·1

A1   BODY PLAN (1/96 scale)

A Lines and general arrangement

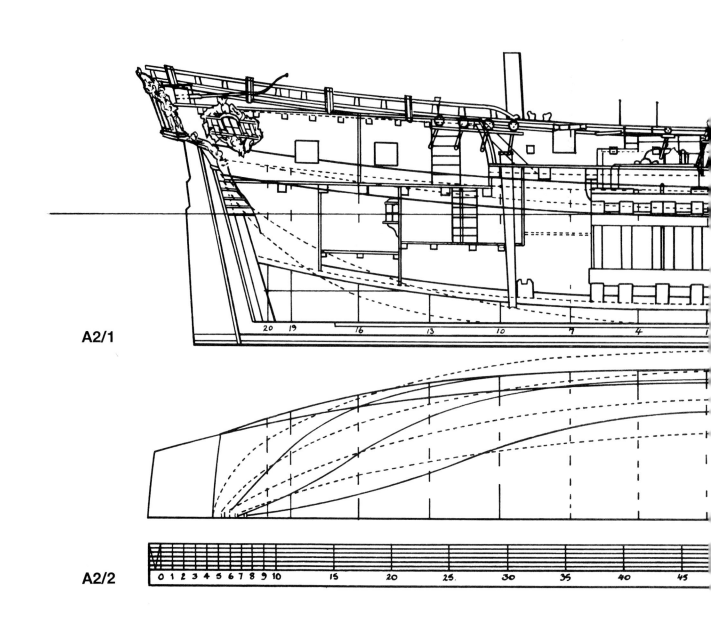

A2/1

A2/2

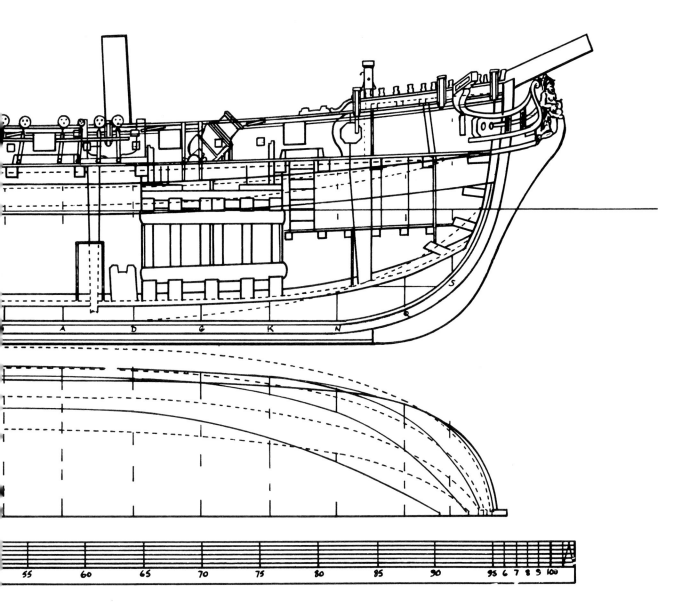

A   D   G   K   N

S

55   60   65   70   75   80   85   90   95 6 7 8 9 100

B Hull construction

B1 BOW (1/96 scale)

B1/1 Stempost and associated timbers, profile

B1/2 Stempost, end view

1. Forecastle
2. Bowsprit
3. Stempost – upper portion
4. Breasthook
5. Bowsprit step
6. Apron (or false stem)
7. Upper deck
8. Upper deck deckhook
9. Breasthook
10. Stemson
11. Platform deck
12. Stem scarph
13. Stempost—lower portion
14. Apron scarph
15. Deadwood
16. Keelson
17. Rising wood
18. Boxing
19. Main keel
20. False keels
21. Hog scarph
22. Hog
23. Fore end of main keel
24. False keel

B1/3 Knee of the head

1. Lacing or collar piece
2. Piece for the figure
3. Hole for main stay collar
4. Chock
5. Slot for gammon lashing
6. Bobstay piece
7. Clench bolts
8. Scarph
9. Stempost
10. Fore end of keel (boxing)
11. Gripe
12. Upper false keel
13. Lower false keel

B1/4 Stempost detail: boxing scarph (1/24 scale)

1. Bolt
2. Bolt holes
3. Lower portion of the stem post
4. Fore portion of main keel
5. False keel (elm)
6. False keel (teak)
7. Tabling of the scarph

B1/5 Stempost detail: stempost scarph (1/24 scale)

1. Bolt
2. Bolt holes
3. Upper portion of stempost
4. Tabling of the scarph
5. Lower portion of stempost

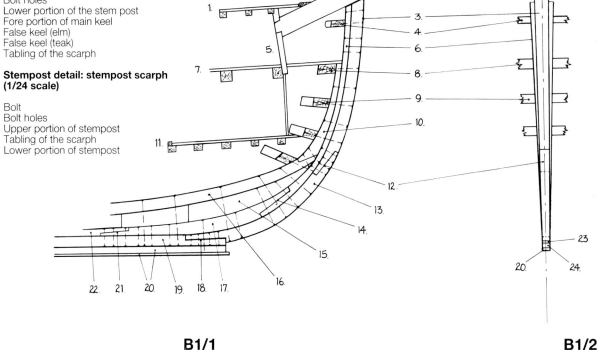

B1/1

B1/2

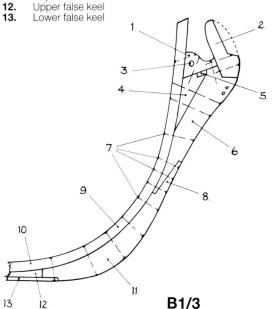

B1/3

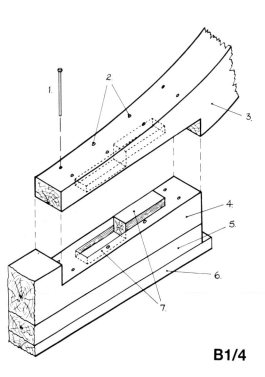

B1/4

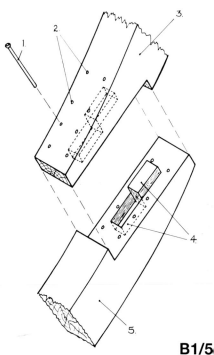

B1/5

44

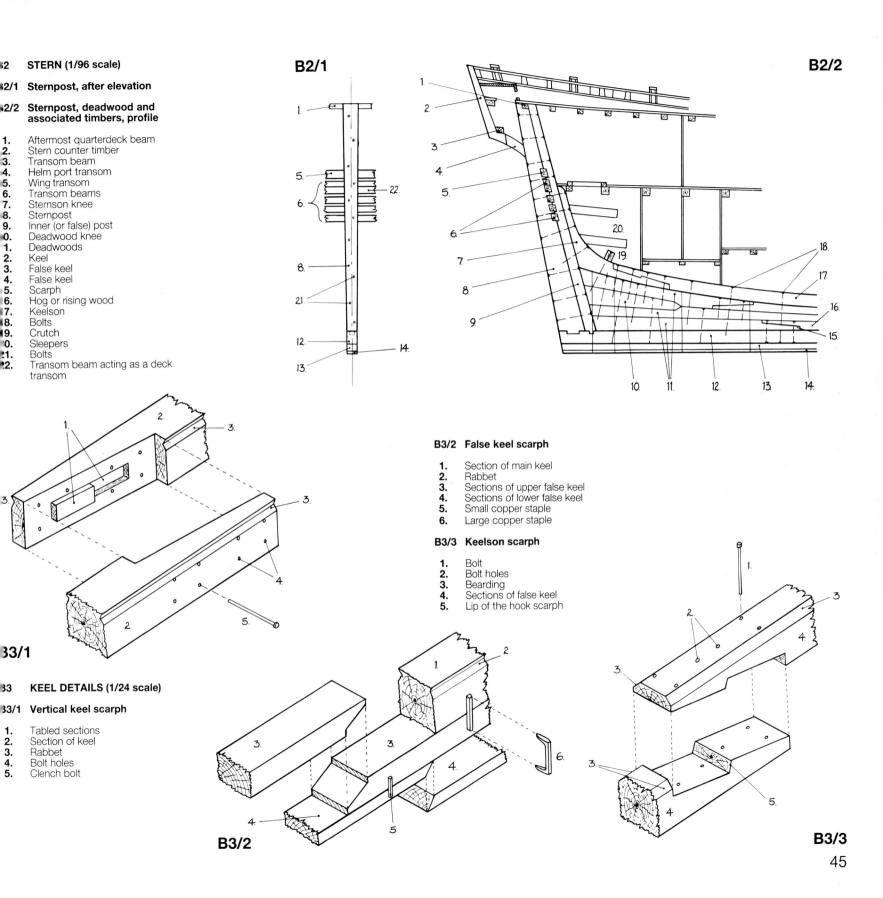

B2   **STERN (1/96 scale)**

B2/1   **Sternpost, after elevation**

B2/2   **Sternpost, deadwood and associated timbers, profile**

1. Aftermost quarterdeck beam
2. Stern counter timber
3. Transom beam
4. Helm port transom
5. Wing transom
6. Transom beams
7. Sternson knee
8. Sternpost
9. Inner (or false) post
10. Deadwood knee
11. Deadwoods
12. Keel
13. False keel
14. False keel
15. Scarph
16. Hog or rising wood
17. Keelson
18. Bolts
19. Crutch
20. Sleepers
21. Bolts
22. Transom beam acting as a deck transom

B2/1

B2/2

B3/2   **False keel scarph**

1. Section of main keel
2. Rabbet
3. Sections of upper false keel
4. Sections of lower false keel
5. Small copper staple
6. Large copper staple

B3/3   **Keelson scarph**

1. Bolt
2. Bolt holes
3. Bearding
4. Sections of false keel
5. Lip of the hook scarph

B3/1

B3   **KEEL DETAILS (1/24 scale)**

B3/1   **Vertical keel scarph**

1. Tabled sections
2. Section of keel
3. Rabbet
4. Bolt holes
5. Clench bolt

B3/2

B3/3

B Hull construction

B4   FRAMING (1/96 scale)

B4/1 Framing elevation, full frames at every room and space

B4/2 Framing plan, full frames at every room and space

1. Quarter badge light lintel
2. Quarter badge light sill
3. Filling toptimber
4. Filling pieces
5. Port sill
6. Inserted timberhead
7. Fife rail
8. Sweep port
9. Planksheer rail
10. Filling lintel
11. Toptimber
12. Lengthening piece
13. Gun port sill
14. Lengthening piece
15. Sweep port sill
16. Canted toptimbers
17. Hance
18. Fife rail
19. Timberheads
20. Position of cathead
21. Knighthead
22. Filling lintel supporting cathead
23. Chase port
24. Hawse holes
25. Hawse pieces
26. Stem post
27. Filling hawse timber
28. Rabbet of the stem post
29. Foremost can frame
30. Fore deadwood
31. Rise of the floors forward
32. First fore cant frame
33. Foremost square frame
34. Floor timbers
35. First futtock timbers
36. Second futtock timbers
37. Third futtock timbers
38. Aftermost square frame
39. Rabbet of the keel
40. Rise of the floors aft
41. First after cant frame
42. Lower false keel (beech)
43. Upper false keel (teak)
44. After deadwood
45. Main keel (elm)
46. Inner (or false) post
47. Stern post
48. Rabbet of the stern post
49. Vertical filling timbers
50. Transom beams
51. Deck transom
52. Transom beam
53. Wing transom
54. Fashion piece—aftermost cant frame
55. Counter timber
56. Filling frames
57. Stern side counter timber
58. Quarter badge light
59. Ports (used as cabin lights)
60. Gun ports
61. Middle counter timber
62. Tie beam
63. Midship counter timber
64. After port
65. After deadwood
66. Line of the floor timber heads

67. Centreline
68. Single frame at the dead flat
69. Line of the first futtock heads
70. Joint lines of double frames
71. Line of the second futtock heads
72. Fore deadwood
73. Apron (or false stem)
74. Head of the apron
75. Bollard timber

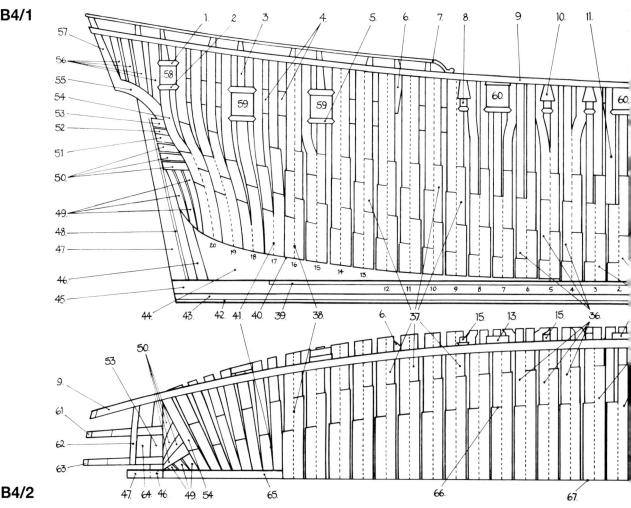

B4/1

B4/2

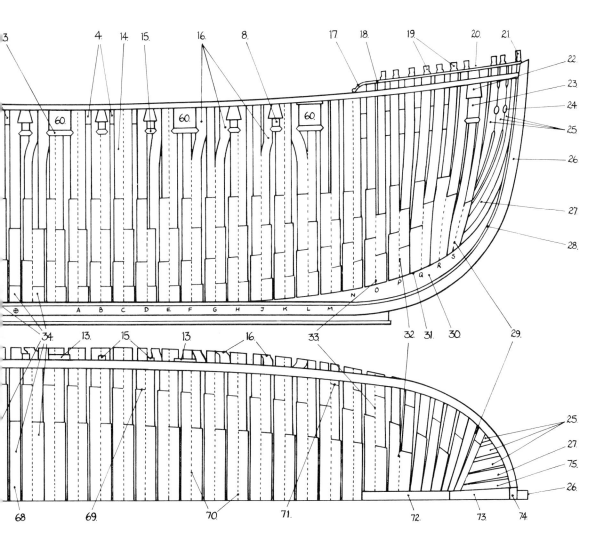

B Hull construction

B4/3 Framing elevation, full frames at every third room and space, with single filling frames between

B4/4 Framing plan, full frames at every third room and space, with three single filling frames between

1. Side cast lengthening piece
2. Filling pieces
3. Toptimbers
4. Lengthening pieces
5. Planksheer rail
6. Filling timber
7. Canted toptimber
8. Filling pieces
9. Stem port
10. Foremost cant frame
11. Foremost square frame
12. Second futtocks
13. Keel
14. Main frame joint line
15. Floor timbers
16. First futtocks
17. Main square frame
18. Single filling frames
19. Third futtocks
20. Aftermost square frame
21. Stern post
22. Fashion piece

All other components are as indicated in drawings B4/1 and B4/2

B4/3

B4/4

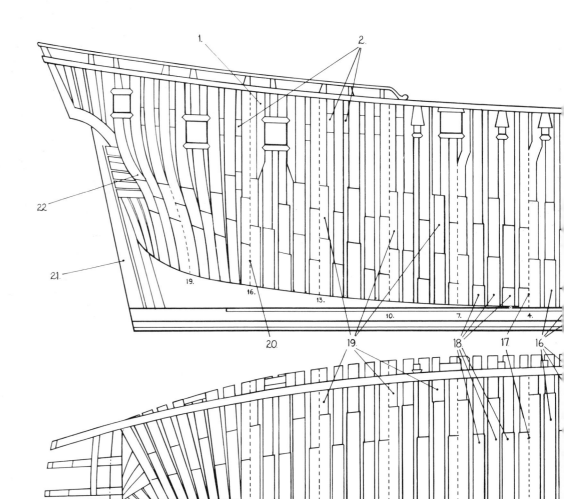

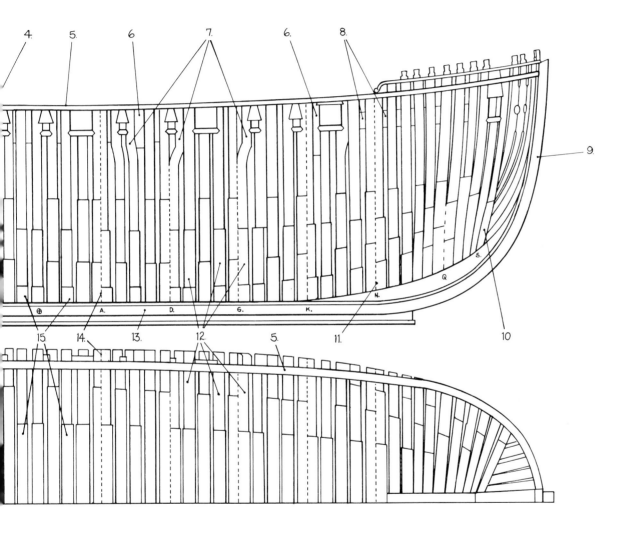

B Hull construction

B4/5 Midship timbers isometric projection (no scale)

1. Gunport sill
2. Toptimber
3. Filling chock fitted in way of main channel
4. Lengthening piece
5. Recess for upper deck beam end
6. Canted lengthening piece
7. Short toptimber
8. Lengthening piece scarph
9. Third futtocks
10. Second futtocks
11. Anchor or jointing chock
12. First futtocks
13. Heel scarph
14. Floor timbers
15. Anchor or jointing chock
16. Horizontal bolt driven through frames
17. Floor timbers
18. Score in hog to receive floor timbers
19. Seating on hog for cross chock
20. Horizontal bolt holes
21. Joint line of full frame
22. Frame—single frame to permit reversal of floors in fore and after body (symbol ⊕ represents dead flat)
23. Main keel
24. False keels
25. Cross section of cross chock
26. Cross section of floor timber.
27. Hog (or rising wood)
28. Keelson
29. Limberboard (showing hole for lifting)
30. Limber strake
31. Footwaling
32. Bolt—driven through keelson, floor timber and keel
33. Lower strake of thickstuff footwaling
34. Thickstuff over the floor heads and first futtock heads
35. Upper strake of footwaling
36. Recesses to receive mortar pit beams
37. Two strakes of thickstuff
38. Mortar pit beam shelf
39. Single strake of thickstuff
40. Upper deck deck clamp (or beam shelf)
41. Sweep port sill
42. Sweep port lintel fashioned as a filling piece
43. Planksheer rail
44. Cross chock—fitted over hog and across first futtock heels

B4/5

B4/6

B4/7

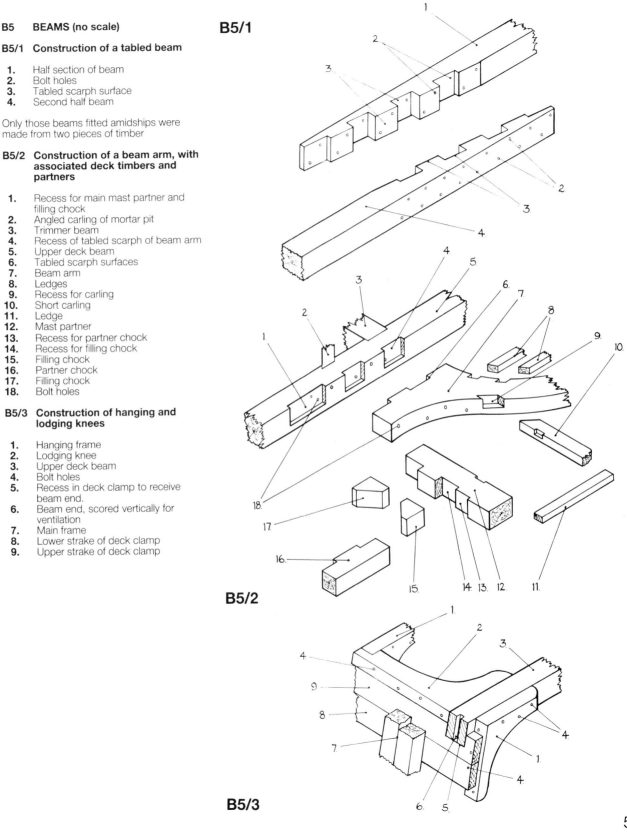

B5 BEAMS (no scale)

B5/1 Construction of a tabled beam

1. Half section of beam
2. Bolt holes
3. Tabled scarph surface
4. Second half beam

Only those beams fitted amidships were made from two pieces of timber

B5/2 Construction of a beam arm, with associated deck timbers and partners

1. Recess for main mast partner and filling chock
2. Angled carling of mortar pit
3. Trimmer beam
4. Recess of tabled scarph of beam arm
5. Upper deck beam
6. Tabled scarph surfaces
7. Beam arm
8. Ledges
9. Recess for carling
10. Short carling
11. Ledge
12. Mast partner
13. Recess for partner chock
14. Recess for filling chock
15. Filling chock
16. Partner chock
17. Filling chock
18. Bolt holes

B5/3 Construction of hanging and lodging knees

1. Hanging frame
2. Lodging knee
3. Upper deck beam
4. Bolt holes
5. Recess in deck clamp to receive beam end.
6. Beam end, scored vertically for ventilation
7. Main frame
8. Lower strake of deck clamp
9. Upper strake of deck clamp

B4/6 Disposition of head timbers (1/96 scale)

B4/7 Disposition of stern timbers (1/96 scale)

1. Starboard timberheads
2. Fife rail
3. Stem post head fashioned to accept bowsprit
4. Knighthead
5. Mooring timberheads
6. Position for cathead
7. Port timberheads
8. Planksheer rail
9. Chase port lintel built solid to support cathead
10. Chase port
11. Chase port sill
12. Joint lines of hawse pieces
13. Joint line of timber 'P'
14. Joint line of timber 'Q'
15. Joint line of timber 'R'
16. Fore edge of timber 'N'
17. Joint line of timber 'O'
18. Foremost square frame
19. Stempost
20. Joint line of foremost cant frame
21. Bollard timber
22. Filling hawse timber
23. Hawse pieces
24. Chase port
25. Hawse holes
26. Stern side canter timber
27. Head of sternpost
28. Midship and middle counter timbers
29. Quarterdeck deck transom
30. Tie beam
31. Counter piece
32. Wing frame
33. After port lintel
34. Fashion piece (aftermost cant frame)
35. Transom beams
36. Sternpost
37. Lower false keel
38. Upper false keel
39. Main keel
40. Vertical filling timbers
41. Transom beam tenoned into fashion piece
42. Deck transom
43. Transom beam
44. After port
45. Dashed line shows helm port

B5/1

B5/2

B5/3

B Hull construction

B6/1

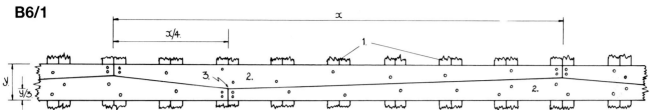

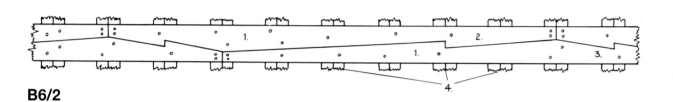

B6/2

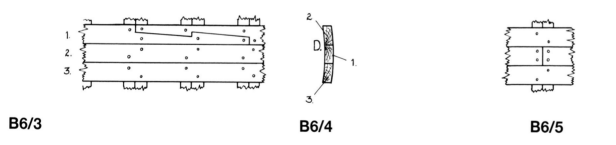

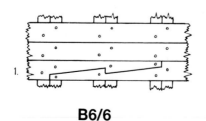

B6/3

B6/4

B6/5

B6/6

B6 **PLANKING TECHNIQUES (1/48 scale)**

B6/1 **Top and butt planking, employed for spirketting, bands of thickstuff and the solid-built main wale**

1. Main timbers (or frames)
2. Single plank, fashioned top and butt
3. The touch of the plank

B6/2 **Hook and butt planking, usually employed for solid-built main wales**

1. Single plank, fashioned hook and butt
2. Long hook scarph
3. Short hook scarph
4. Timbers (or frames)

B6/3 **Detail of main wale**

1. Upper strake of main wale with hook scarph
2. Filling strake (or plank between the wales)
3. Lower strake of the main wale

B6/4 **Cross-section of main wale**

1. Filling strake
2. Upper strake of the main wale
3. Lower strake of the main wale

B6/5 **Butt joint of the filling strake**

B6/6 **Detail of the lower strake of the main wale**

1. Reverse direction hook scarph

B6/7 Methods of securing planking with trennals

1. Timbers (or frames)
2. Single fastening method
3. Double fastening method
4. Combined single and double method

The butt ends of the planks would have been secured with two nails or dumps

B6/8 Dropstrakes and stealers (no scale)

1. Dropstrake
2. Stern post
3. Stealer
4. Hood ends of the planks
5. Rabbet of the stern post
6. Bottom planking

These were worked in at the ends of the bottom planking strakes to reduce 'sny' at the hood ends. Either or both were employed as required. They were also used for planking the stem of the ship

B6/9 Hook and butt anchor stock planking, used for deck clamps

1. Hook
2. Upper deck beams
3. Lip of the hook
4. Butt joint
5. Recess or score to receive beam end
6. Lower strake of clamp
7. Upper strake of clamp

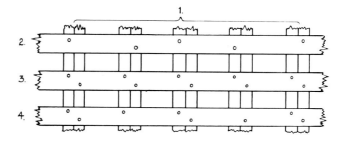

B6/7

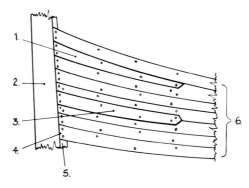

B6/8

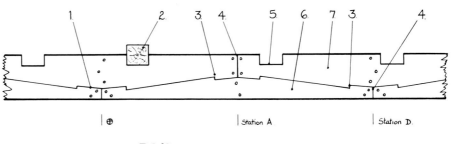

B6/9

53

C Internal hull

C1 GENERAL ARRANGEMENT

C1/1 Longitudinal section (1/96 scale)

1. Housing over the rudder head
2. Swivel gun pedestal
3. Tiller
4. Sheave block
5. Kevel
6. Ladder to quarter deck
7. Mizzen mast
8. Timberheads
9. Entry port stanchions
10. Mortar pit cover
11. Oar ports
12. Cleat
13. Main jeer bitts
14. Main mast
15. Main topsail bitts
16. Fish davit cleat
17. Belfry
18. Galley flue
19. Cathead
20. Bowsprit
21. Figurehead
22. Slot for gammon lashing
23. Hawse holes
24. Bowsprit step
25. Windlass
26. Gunport
27. Hatchway to fore platform
28. Mortar pit
29. Mortar
30. Mortar bed
31. Main hatch
32. Spirketting
33. Entry port ladder
34. Quarterdeck bulkhead
35. Lieutenant's cabin
36. Spirketting
37. Captain's day cabin
38. Wing transom knee
39. Quarter light
40. Rudder head
41. Stern counter timber
42. Wing transom
43. Transom beams
44. Deck clamp
45. Sleepers
46. Bread room
47. Filling room of magazine
48. Lobby to magazine
49. Door to magazine
50. Surgeon's cabin
51. Purser's cabin
52. Hanging knee
53. After hold
54. After shell room
55. Deck clamp
56. Bilge pump
57. Lobby
58. Galley
59. Firehearth
60. Copper kettle
61. Forepeak and boatswain's store
62. Knee of the head
63. Stem post
64. Apron or false stem
65. Breast hooks
66. Stemson
67. Void space
68. Coal hole
69. Fore shell room
70. Centreline stanchion

71. Lobby
72. Steward's bedplace and store
73. Rope stowage
74. Crutch
75. Sternson knee
76. Rudder
77. Sternpost
78. Inner or false post
79. Deadwood
80. Elm tree pump (sea suction)
81. Mizzen mast step
82. Keel
83. Riders
84. Keelson
85. False keels
86. Pump well
87. Main mast step
88. Riders
89. Boxing
90. Gripe

C1/1

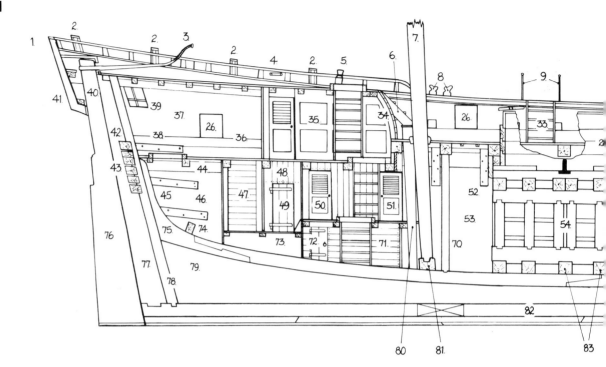

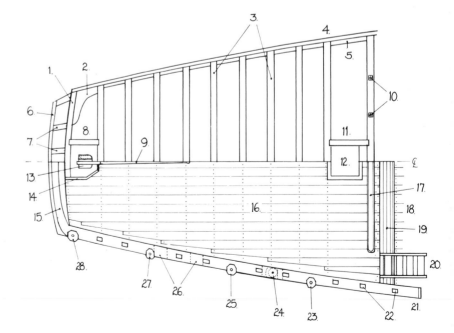

C2/1

54

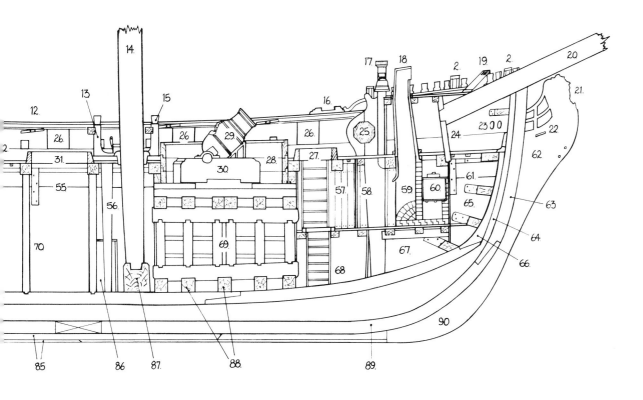

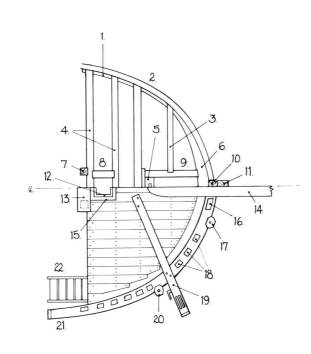

C2 QUARTERDECK AND FORECASTLE (1/96 scale)

C2/1 Quarterdeck plan

1. Deck transom
2. Transom knee
3. Deck beams
4. Frame moulding line
5. Deck clamp
6. Tafferal
7. Stern counter timbers
8. Carling
9. Tiller
10. Breast rail pillars
11. Carling
12. Companionway
13. Rudder head
14. Rudder head housing
15. Fiferail
16. Deck planking
17. Breast rail
18. Upper deck
19. Transverse bulkhead
20. Ladder
21. Fiferail hance
22. Timberheads
23. Swivel gun pedestal
24. Sheave block
25. Swivel gun pedestal
26. Fairleads
27. Swivel gun pedestal
28. Swivel gun pedestal

C2/2 Forecastle plan

1. Deck clamp
2. Frame moulding line
3. Half beam
4. Deck beam
5. Bowsprit step
6. Deck hook
7. Belfry pillar
8. Carling
9. Carling
10. Apron
11. Stemson
12. Galley flue
13. Belfry canopy
14. Bowsprit
15. Coaming
16. Knighthead
17. Swivel gun pedestal
18. Timberheads
19. Cathead
20. Swivel gun pedestal
21. Fiferail
22. Ladder

C2/2

C Internal hull

C3 MAIN DECK AND CABIN DECK
(1/96 scale)

C3/1

C3/1 Main (or upper) deck plan

1. Lodging knee
2. Deck beam
3. Hanging knee
4. Angled carling
5. Angled bulkhead
6. Heavy longitudinal carling (trimmer beam)
7. Half beam
8. Mortar pit housing
9. Mortar pit outboard bulkhead
10. After mortar pit
11. Upper deck beam
12. Mortar pit transverse bulkhead
13. Beam arm
14. Main hatch carling
15. Double lodging knee
16. Main hatchway
17. Beam arm
18. Elm tree pump
19. Partner chock
20. Mast partner
21. Filling chock
22. Half beam
23. Fore mortar pit
24. Trimmer beam
25. Hanging knee
26. Lodging knee
27. Fore access hatch
28. Quarter beam
29. Windlass carrick bitt
30. Belfry pillar
31. Foremost beam
32. Foremost gunport (if fitted)
33. Ekeing
34. Hawse holes
35. Deck hook
36. Apron
37. Stempost
38. Rabbet
39. Heel of bowsprit step
40. The shutting in
41. Bowsprit step
42. Manger bulkhead
43. Plank joggle
44. Foremost gunport (if fitted)
45. Galley flue
46. Standard
47. Belfry pillar
48. Iron pawl
49. Carrick bitt
50. Windlass spindle
51. Fore hatch coaming
52. Mortar pit canopy
53. Mortar pit outboard bulkhead
54. Moulding line
55. Mortar pit waterway
56. Housing cover
57. Main topsail bitts
58. Main mast
59. Elm tree pump
60. Sweep port
61. Main jeer bitts
62. Gunport
63. Main hatch cover
64. Binding strakes
65. Waterway
66. Mortar pit canopy
67. Entry ladder
68. Sweep port

69. Flat of the deck
70. Gunport
71. Sweep port
72. Line of the timbers
73. Quarterdeck ladder
74. Quarterdeck bulkhead
75. Pump handle
76. Elm tree pump
77. Mizzen mast
78. Filling chock
79. Mast partner
80. Elm tree pump
81. Carling (midship tier)
82. Carling (outer tier)
83. Ledges
84. Aftermost upper deck beam
85. Moulding line

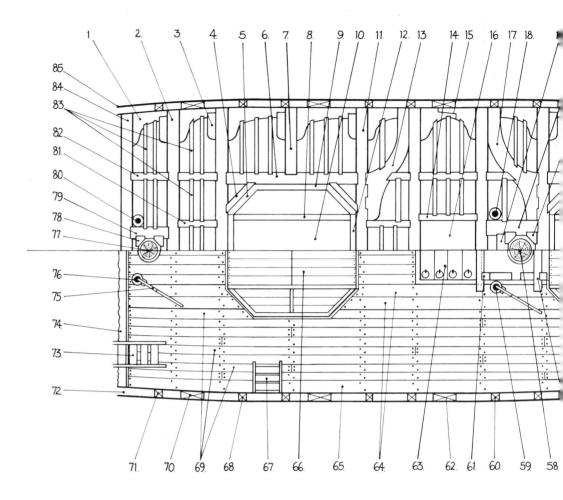

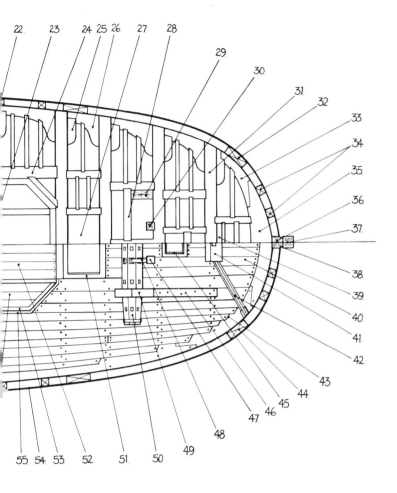

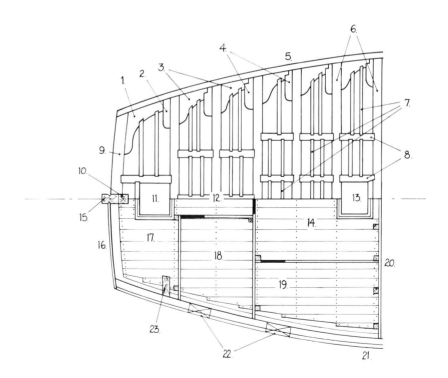

C3/2

C Internal hull

C4/1

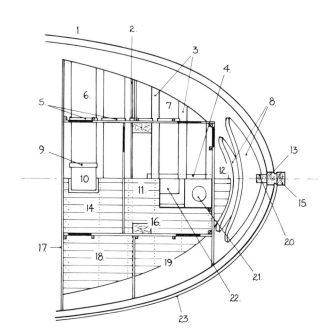

C4 HOLD AND PLATFORMS (1/96 scale)

C4/1 Fore platform plan

1. Frame moulding line
2. Transverse bulkhead below platform
3. Platform beams
4. Heavy carling, supporting firehearth
5. Carlings
6. Boatswain's cabin
7. Sail room
8. Breast hooks
9. Carling
10. Scuttle to coal hole
11. Galley
12. Boatswain's storeroom
13. Apron
14. Lobby
15. Stempost
16. Lower portion of carrick bitt
17. After bulkhead
18. Carpenter's cabin
19. Carpenter's storeroom
20. Stemson
21. Galley boiler
22. Galley firehearth
23. External planking

C4/2 Fore platform isometric section (no scale)

1. Frame (station K)
2. Hanging knee
3. Lodging knee
4. Boatswain's cabin
5. Access door (omitted) to galley
6. Division bulkhead
7. Quarter beam
8. Sail room
9. Galley firehearth
10. Galley flue
11. Access door (omitted) to boatswain's storeroom
12. Ekeing
13. Fore transverse bulkhead
14. Carling
15. Deck hook
16. Hawse timbers
17. Stemson
18. Apron
19. Stem post
20. Boatswain's storeroom
21. Galley stove
22. Carpenter's storeroom
23. Rabbet for ledge
24. External hull planking
25. Carrick bitt pin
26. Galley transverse bulkhead (partially omitted for clarity)
27. Carpenter's cabin
28. Mortar pit beam shelf
29. Ceiling
30. After bulkhead (partially omitted for clarity)
31. Coal hole
32. Scuttle to coal hole
33. Platform lobby
34. Main keel
35. Keelson
36. Floor rider
37. Timber (or frame)
38. Shell room longitudinal support beams
39. Thick stuff
40. Futtock rider
41. Mortar pit beam
42. Deck clamp
43. External planking
44. Upper deck beam

C4/2

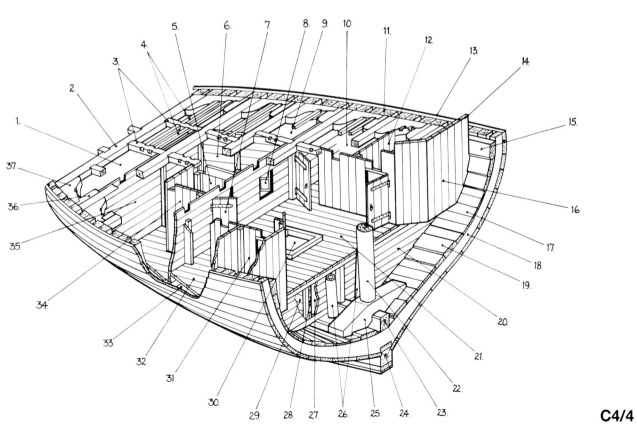

C4/3 After platform plan

1. Carlings
2. Frame moulding line
3. Breadroom
4. Purser's cabin
5. Surgeon's cabin
6. Magazine deck beams
7. Light box
8. Steward's room (below platform)
9. Platform beams
10. Elm tree pump (sea suction)
11. Filling room
12. Lobby (both above and below platform deck)
13. Hatchway
14. Carling
15. Mizzen mast
16. After bulkhead magazine
17. Elm tree pump (sea suction)
18. Powder room
19. Marine officer's cabin
20. Gunner's cabin
21. External planking

C4/3

C4/4 After platform isometric section (no scale)

1. Bread room
2. Cabin deck beam
3. Carling
4. Ledges
5. Magazine door
6. Filling room
7. Access door to magazine
8. Light box
9. Bread room wing
10. Purser's cabin
11. Frame
12. Surgeon's cabin
13. Outer planking
14. Bulkhead extension to upper deck
15. Deck clamp
16. Cabin fore bulkhead
17. Lining
18. Frame
19. Thickstuff
20. Fore bulkhead of lower rooms
21. After platform lobby
22. Mizzen mast
23. Keelson
24. Keel
25. Mast step
26. Elm tree pump casings
27. Lower room lobby
28. Fore and aft bulkhead
29. Captain's storeroom (steward's room opposite side)
30. Hatchway
31. Gunner's cabin
32. Marine officer's cabin
33. After end of captain's store
34. Magazine lobby
35. Main magazine (powder room)
36. Hanging knee
37. Lodging knee

C4/4

C Internal hull

C5/1

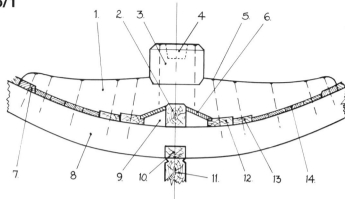

C5/2

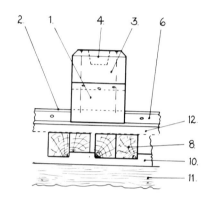

C5	MAST STEPS (1/48 scale)
C5/1	Mainmast step cross-section
C5/2	Mainmast step side elevation
C5/3	Mainmast step isometric projection (no scale)

1. Rider supporting step
2. Keelson
3. Step baulk
4. Mortice to receive mast tenon
5. Clench bolt
6. Limber board
7. Thickstuff over the floorheads
8. Frame (or timber)
9. Limber passage
10. Hog
11. Keel
12. Limber strake
13. Footwaling (or strake next to the limberstrake)
14. Ceiling

C5/4	Mizzen mast step cross-section
C5/5	Mizzen mast step side elevation

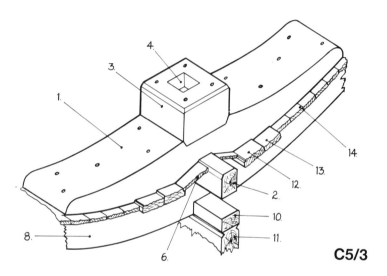

C5/3

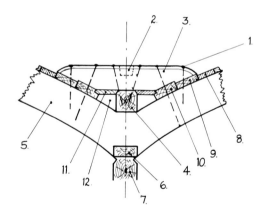

C5/4

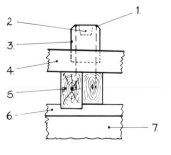

C5/5

60

5/6 Mizzen mast step isometric projection (no scale)

1. Clench bolt
2. Mortice to receive mast tenon
3. Mast step
4. Keelson
5. Frame (or timber)
6. Hog
7. Keel
8. Ceiling
9. Footwaling
10. Limber strake
11. Limber board
12. Limber passage

5/7 Bowsprit step isometric projection (no scale)

1. Forecastle beam
2. Mortice for carling
3. Bolts
4. Carling
5. Half beam
6. Step baulk
7. Upper deck planking
8. Ledge
9. Bolt
10. Step recessed into beam
11. Upper deck beam
12. Forelock bolt
13. Step baulk
14. Mortice to receive bowsprit heel

C6 BULKHEADS (1/96 scale)

C6/1 Quarterdeck bulkhead front elevation

1. Foot rail
2. Pillar
3. Breastrail balustrade
4. Quarterdeck planking
5. Ship's side
6. Upper deck planking
7. Waterway
8. Panels
9. Half doors to cabin accommodation
10. Curved pillar (stiffener)

C6/2 Alternative form of quarterdeck bulkhead, front elevation and section

1. Quarterdeck planking
2. Half doors to cabin accommodation
3. Ladder
4. Upper deck planking
5. Bulkhead planking
6. Deep waterway
7. Quarter deck beams
8. Upper deck planking
9. Aftermost upper deck beam
10. Bulkhead vertical stiffener

C6/3 Captain's accommodation bulkhead front elevation

1. Quarterdeck planking
2. Ship's side
3. Recessed panels
4. Cabin deck planking
5. Bulkhead retaining sill
6. Door to captain's accommodation
7. Portable sections of bulkhead

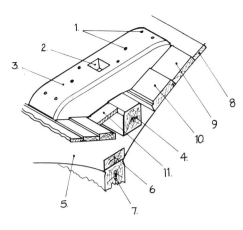

C5/6

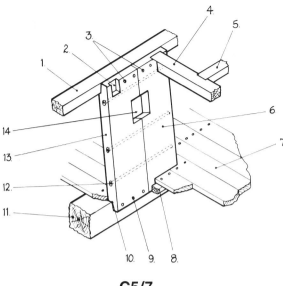

C5/7

C6/2

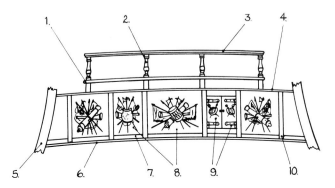

C6/1

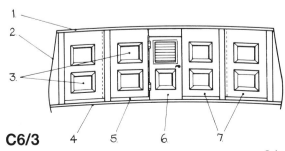

C6/3

C Internal hull

C6/4 Captain's berth after bulkhead, after elevation

1. Pillar
2. Portable panel
3. Ship's side

C6/5 Captain's berth longitudinal bulkhead, internal elevation

1. Recess for quarterdeck beams
2. Captain's accommodation bulkhead (section)
3. Pillar
4. Recessed panels
5. Bulkhead retaining sills
6. Cabin deck planking
7. Doorway to captain's day cabin

C6/6 Lieutenant's cabin bulkhead elevation (master's cabin opposite)

1. Recess for quarterdeck beams
2. Louvred panel of door
3. Pillar
4. Cabin entry door
5. Cabin deck planking
6. Portable panel
7. Bulkhead retaining sills
8. Transverse plank below upper deck beam
9. Curve of bulkhead to conform to quarterdeck bulkhead

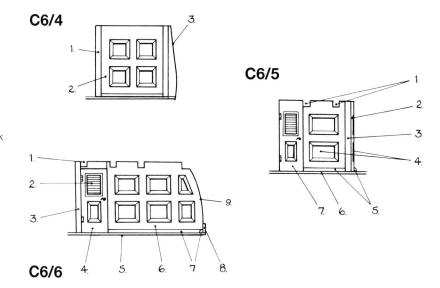

C6/4

C6/5

C6/6

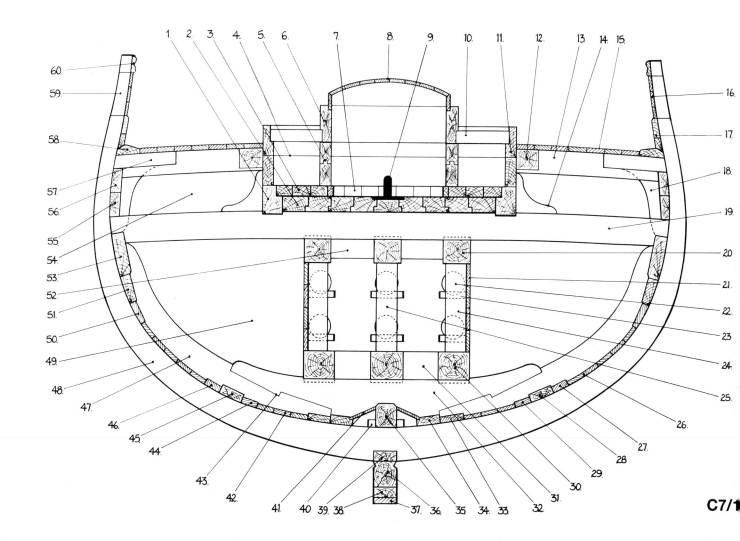

C7/1

C7 MORTAR PIT AND SHELL ROOM (1/48 scale)

C7/1 After mortar pit and shell room. cross-section

1. Mortar pit longitudinal boundary timber
2. Mortar pit planking, cyphered together
3. Secondary planking, 9in wide
4. Joint line of mortar pit boundary bulkheads
5. Removable longitudinal housing, rabbeted together
6. Mortar pit housing, removable
7. Mortar bed turntable base well
8. Canopy
9. Turntable spindle
10. Removable strongback
11. Mortar pit outboard bulkhead
12. Heavy longitudinal carling (trimmer beam)
13. Upper deck beam
14. Mortar pit support standard
15. Flat of the upper deck
16. Lining
17. Spirketting
18. Hanging knee
19. Mortar pit beam
20. Longitudinal support beam
21. Shell room bulkhead planking
22. Shell
23. Shell rack
24. Pillar
25. Centreline pillar
26. Ceiling
27. Upper strake of footwaling
28. Thickstuff
29. Lower strake of footwaling
30. Shell room longitudinal support beam
31. Filling timber
32. Floor rider
33. Footwaling
34. Limber strake
35. Keelson
36. Keel
37. False keel (lower)
38. False keel (upper)
39. Hog
40. Limber hole
41. Limber board
42. Ceiling
43. Floor rider scarph
44. Lower strake of footwaling
45. Thick stuff
46. Upper strake of footwaling
47. Futtock rider
48. Frame (or timber)
49. Hold
50. Thickstuff
51. Thickstuff, upper strake
52. Filling timber
53. Deck clamp
54. Void space*
55. Lower strake of upper deck beam shelf
56. Upper strake of upper deck beam shelf
57. Lodging knee
58. Waterway
59. Gunport
60. Sheer rail

* It seems likely that the mortar pit support beams were planked over in this area, the compartment thus formed being used for stores

C7/2 After mortar pit and shell room. longitudinal section

1. Canopy cover
2. Dashed line shows division between the angled and outboard mortar pit bulkheads
3. Canopy (shown in its sliding position)
4. Iron spindle
5. Removable strongback
6. Removable longitudinal housing— upper and lower strakes
7. Canopy in closed position
8. Rabbet
9. Mortar pit transverse bulkhead
10. Upper deck planking
11. Upper deck beam
12. Filling support timber
13. Transverse covering timber
14. Mortar pit support beam
15. Space between beams
16. Longitudinal support beam
17. Pillars
18. Shell
19. Shell rack
20. Dashed line shows shell room deck
21. Shell room longitudinal support beam
22. Keelson
23. Station line of timbers
24. Main keel
25. Upper false keel
26. Lower false keel
27. Dashed line shows hog
28. Dashed line shows lower edge of floor riders
29. Floor rider
30. Shell room deck beam
31. Pillar heel tenon
32. Facing plank
33. Pillar head tenon
34. Filling timber
35. Mortar pit planking, primary
36. Turntable base well
37. Secondary planking
38. Rabbet
39. Dashed lines show rabbet to receive side covers
40. Canopy transom

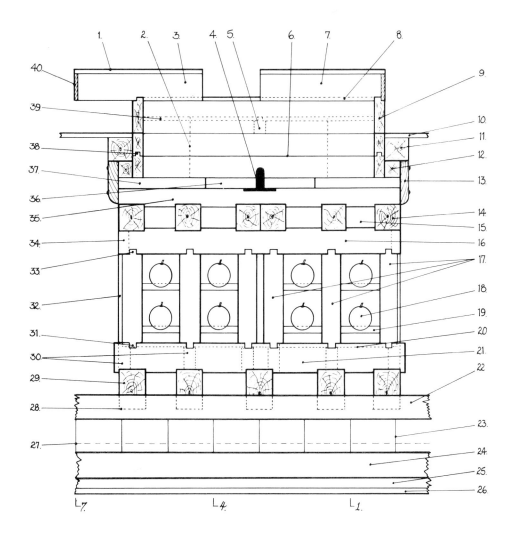

C7/2

63

C Internal hull

C7/3 **Plan of mortar pit housing: upper deck (left) and above deck (right)**

1. Hanging knee
2. Upper deck beam, aftermost
3. Lodging knee
4. Mortar pit housing, removable
5. Rabbet
6. Mortar pit outboard bulkhead
7. Half beam
8. Line shows deck clamp
9. Lodging knee
10. Secondary planking
11. Inboard line of ship's timbers
12. Hanging knee
13. Upper deck beam, foremost
14. Ledge
15. Angled carling
16. Carling, side tier
17. Beam arm
18. Tabled scarph
19. Carling, midship tier
20. Perimeter of turntable base well
21. Primary planking of mortar pit
22. Flange of spindle
23. Spindle
24. Shutting-in planking
25. Binding strakes
26. Angled bulkhead
27. Sliding canopy
28. Void space*
29. Flat of the upper deck
30. Rabbet
31. Mortar pit housing, removable
32. Mortar pit outboard bulkhead
33. Strongback, supporting housing covers (removable)
34. Housing cover
35. Housing cover lifting ringbolt
36. Sliding canopy
37. First strake of the flat of the deck
38. Binding strake
39. Mortice to receive strongback
40. King plank
41. Centreline carling
42. After bulkhead, removable
43. Rabbet for canopy
44. Dashed line shows boundary of removable housing
45. Angled bulkhead
46. Angled carling
47. Ledge
48. Carling, side tier
49. Heavy longitudinal carling (trimmer beam)
50. Ledges

* Used as a storage space when mortar not in use, for mortar stores

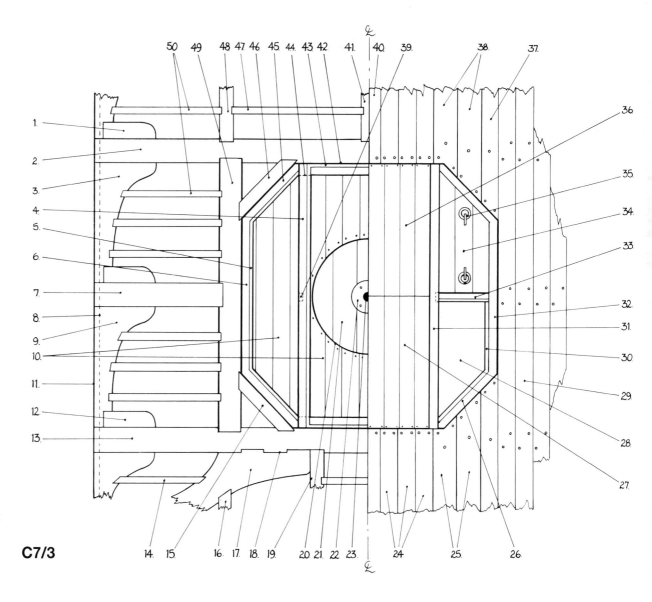

C7/3

7/4 Plan or mortar pit deck (right) and support beams (left)

1. Inboard line of the ship's timbers
2. Deck clamp supporting mortar pit beams
3. Intermediate support beam
4. Line shows positioning of standards
5. Longitudinal support beam, centreline
6. Perimeter of turntable base well
7. After bulkhead
8. Secondary planking (9in wide)
9. Filling support timber
10. Angled bulkhead
11. Transverse covering timber
12. Mortar pit longitudinal boundary timber
13. Dashed line shows position of upper deck beams
14. Aftermost support beam
15. Mortar pit support standards
16. Support beams, middle tiers
17. Mortar pit outboard bulkhead
18. Mortar pit longitudinal boundary timber, lower portion
19. Bolts, horizontal
20. Primary planking of mortar pit, 12in wide, cyphered together
21. Flange of spindle
22. Spindle
23. Longitudinal support beam, outboard
24. Joint position longitudinal and transverse beams
25. Foremost support beam
26. Dashed line shows position of upper deck beam

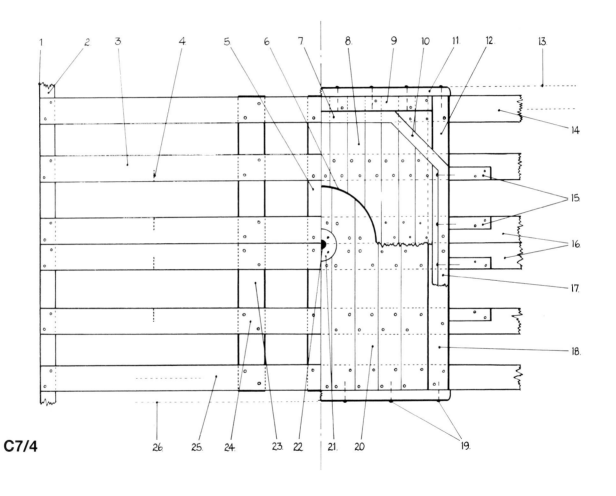

C7/4

65

C Internal hull

C7/5 Plan showing construction, support and layout of shell room

1. Floor rider
2. Scarph
3. Thickstuff
4. Footwaling
5. Shell room bulkhead planking, 2in thick
6. Pillar
7. Pillar heel tenon
8. Shell room longitudinal support beam
9. Shell room deck beam, rabbeted on upper edge to receive planks
10. Shell room deck planking
11. Filling timber, rabbeted to receive planks
12. Keelson
13. Shell in its stowed position
14. Upper filling timber
15. Shell rack
16. Longitudinal support beam
17. Floor rider
18. Dashed line shows shell room bulkhead planking below longitudinal
19. Passageway
20. Pillar
21. Futtock rider, partially omitted
22. Longitudinal support beam omitted at this point for clarity
23. Shell room bulkhead planking
24. Dashed line shows futtock rider
25. Floor rider
26. Facing plank
27. Access door
28. Facing plank, partially omitted
29. Centreline pillar
30. Limber board
31. Concave bed formed in shell rack to receive shell
32. Limber strake
33. Footwaling
34. Area of ceiling
35. Lip of scarph
36. Scarph face of futtock rider
37. Footwaling
38. Area of ceiling
39. Limber passage
40. Joint division of floor and futtock riders
41. Limber hole
42. Thickstuff, lower strake
43. Mortice to receive pillar heel tenon
44. Thickstuff, upper strake
45. Floor rider
46. Deck clamp, to support mortar pit beams
47. Inboard line of ship's timbers

Note that components have been omitted in places for clarity

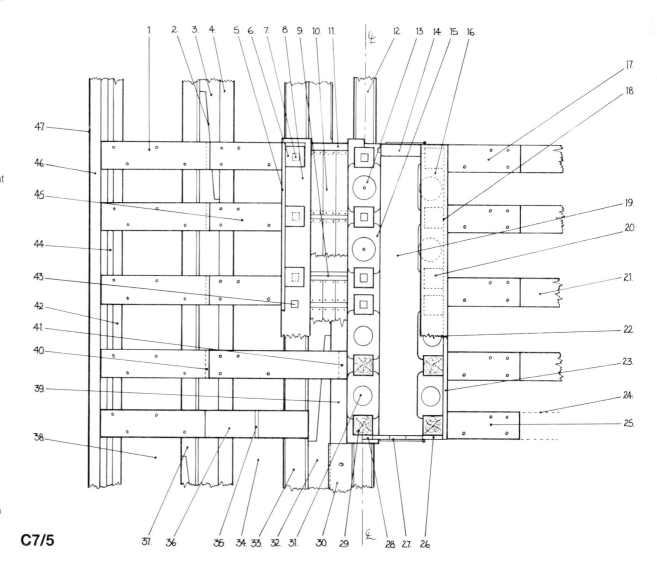

C7/5

7/6   Detail of shell room doors

7/6   Detail of shell room doors

1. Mortar pit beam
2, Filling timber
3. Vertical facing plank
4. Longitudinal support beam
5. Shell room bulkhead planking
6. Upper door
7. Facing plank
8. Hinge pieces
9. Hinge pintles
10. Lower door
11. Floor rider
12. Shell room longitudinal support beam
13. Lower filling timber

C7/6

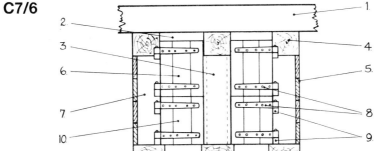

C7/7   Mortar in stowed position, longitudinal section and cross-section

1. Mortar pit transverse bulkhead
2. Canopy side
3. Canopy cover
4. Fore and aft canopy division point
5. Mortar bed
6. Mortar
7. Removable longitudinal housing
8. Canopy transom
9. Lower longitudinal housing (removable)
10. Mortar pit support beam
11. Mortar pit planking (primary)
12. Iron spindle
13. Mortar bed turntable base
14. Secondary planking
15. Removable strongback
16. Canopy rabbet line
17. Rabbet to receive side covers
18. Void space, used for storage when mortar not in use

C7/7

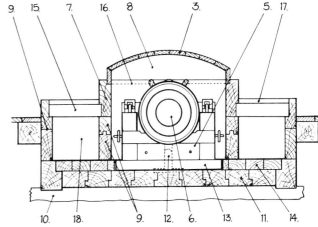

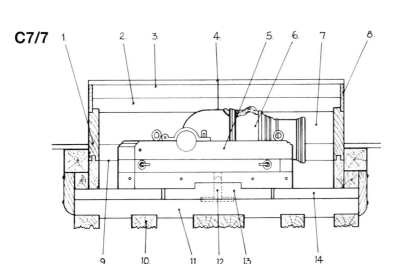

C7/8

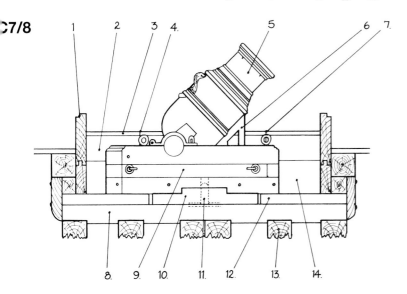

C7/8   Mortar in firing position, longitudinal section

1. Mortar pit transverse bulkhead
2. Mortar pit angled bulkhead, upper strake
3. Rabbet to receive side covers
4. Division line between the angled and outboard mortar pit bulkheads
5. Mortar
6. Mortar support (set at an angle of 45 degrees)
7. Division line between the outboard and angled mortar pit bulkheads
8. Mortar pit planking (primary)
9. Mortar bed
10. Mortar bed turntable base
11. Iron spindle
12. Secondary planking
13. Mortar pit support beam
14. Mortar pit angled bulkhead, lower strake

The mortar is shown facing forward; its correct direction for firing would have been either to port or starboard, or any given angle between the masts

67

D External hull

D1 GENERAL ARRANGEMENT
(1/96 scale)

D1/1 External hull features, aft

1. Tafferal
2. Ship's side planking
3. Swivel gun pedestal
4. Sheer rail
5. Rough tree rail
6. Sheave block
7. Kevel

8. Chain
9. Mizzen channel
10. Deadeye
11. Mizzen mast
12. Kevel cleat
13. Gun port
14. Iron stanchion
15. Entry port ladder
16. Main topmast stay deadeye and stool
17. Main channel
18. Sweep port
19. Lower false keel

20. Scupper
21. Ship's side planking
22. Rabbet line of keel
23. Butt joint of planking
24. Hook and butt scarph
25. Upper main wale
26. Lower main wale
27. Filling wale
28. False keel
29. Gunport lids
30. Main keel
31. Gudgeon brace

32. Stern post
33. Sole of the rudder
34. Rudder
35. Pintle brace
36. Pintle
37. Counter
38. Lower finishing figure
39. Quarter light (badge)
40. Quarter figure
41. Stern lights
42. Cove

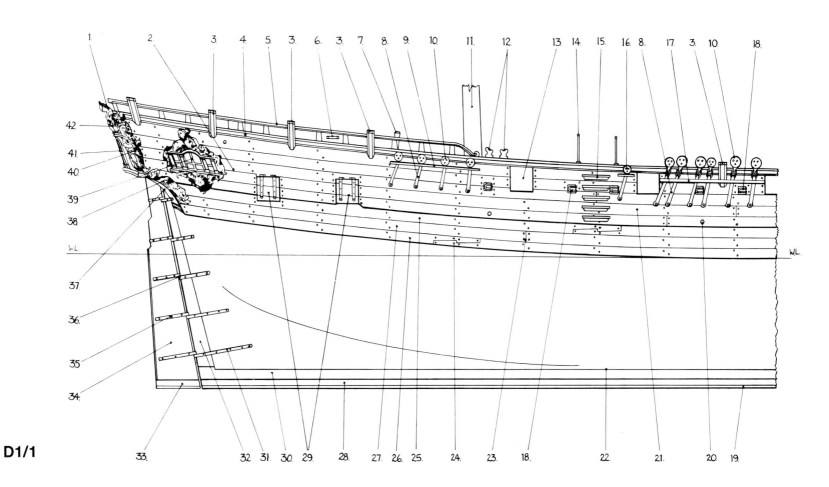

D1/1

1/2 External hull features, forward

1. Deadeye
2. Swivel gun pedestal
3. Main mast
4. Gunport
5. Fenders
6. Sweep port
7. Fish davit cleat
8. Anchor lining
9. Belfry
10. Timberheads

11. Swivel gun pedestal
12. Cat supporter knee
13. Cathead
14. Swivel gun pedestal
15. Knighthead
16. Head rail
17. Bowsprit
18. Figurehead
19. Hair bracket
20. Head timber
21. Gammoning slot
22. Trailboard

23. Knee of the head
24. Hawse holes and lining
25. Cheeks
26. Foremost gunport (if fitted)
27. Stempost
28. Rabbet line
29. Gripe
30. Butt joint of planking
31. Fore foot
32. Boxing
33. Hook and butt scarph
34. Lower false keel

35. False keel
36. Main keel
37. Rabbet line of keel
38. Lower main wale
39. Filling wale
40. Upper main wale
41. Ship's side planking
42. Chain
43. Main channel
44. Scupper

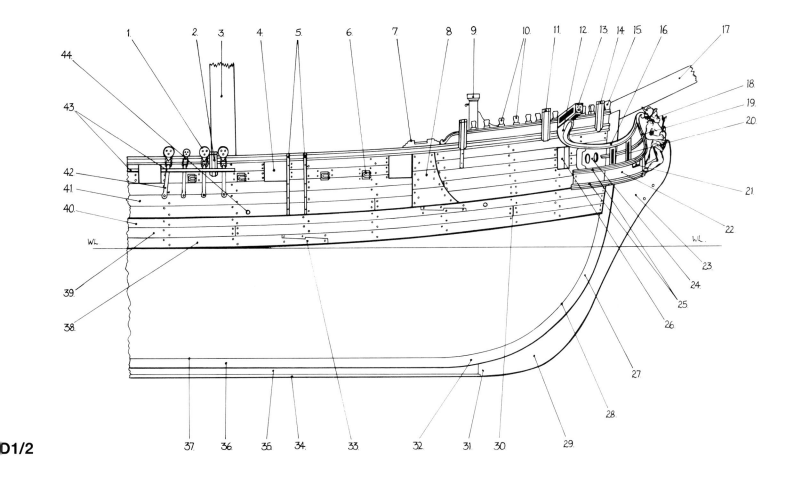

D1/2

D External hull

D2 FIGUREHEAD AND DECORATION
(1/96 scale)

D2/1 Stern decoration

D2/2 Quarter badge

1. Tafferal
2. Roman figures
3. Dragon
4. Quarter figure
5. Lower finishing in the form of a dolphin
6. Counter
7. After port
8. Counter rail
9. Stern lights
10. Cove
11. Upper finishing in the form of a crown
12. Cherubs
13. Quarter light
14. Phoenix

D2/3 Detail of the head (no scale)

1. Cathead
2. Bowsprit
3. Hair bracket
4. Figurehead (Hermes carrying a mortar in his right hand and a winged sceptre in his left)
5. Knee of the head
6. Lower head rail
7. Trailboard
8. Lower cheek
9. Upper cheek
10. Head timbers
11. Main head rail
12. Cathead knee

Note that all figures with the exception of the cherubs carry a mortar shell

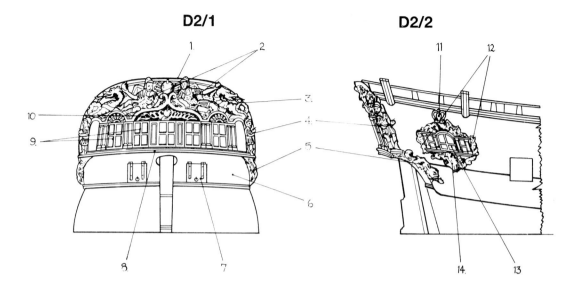

D2/1   **D2/2**

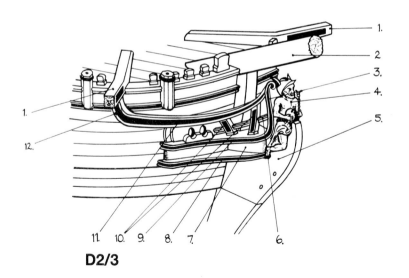

D2/3

D3 EXTERNAL HULL DETAILS

D3/1 Anchor lining detail, isometric projection (no scale)

1. Planksheer
2. Ship's side planking
3. Anchor lining (elm)
4. Blackstrake
5. Upper strake of main wale
6. Filling strake
7. Lower strake of mail wale

D3/2 Chesstrees detail, cross-section and side elevation (1/48 scale)

1. Swivel gun pedestal
2. Forecastle planksheer raii
3. Sheave
4. Sheave pin
5. Sheave slot
6. Chesstree

D3/3 Entry steps and ladder details, cross-section and side elevations (1/48 scale)

1. Ladder tread
2. Ladder style
3. Stanchion
4. Planksheer
5. Entry step
6. Upper deck planking
7. Ship's side planking
8. Blackstrake
9. Upper strake of main wale

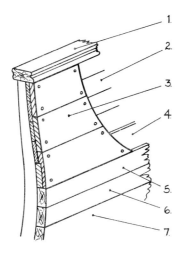

D3/1

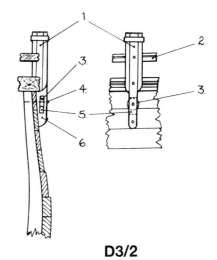

D3/2

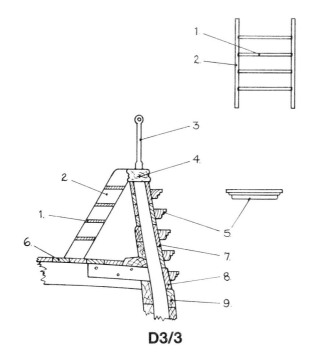

D3/3

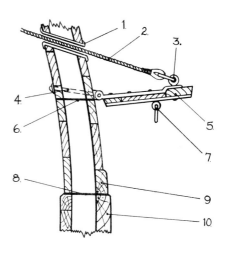

D3/4

71

D External hull

D3/4 Cabin deck port cross-section (1/24 scale)

D3/5 Port cover external elevation (1/24 scale)

D3/6 Port cover section (1/24 scale)

D3/7 Port cover internal elevation (1/24 scale)

1. Lead lining to lead port cover tackle halyard
2. Port cover tackle halyard
3. Eyebolt and ring
4. Pintle securing bolt
5. Port cover
6. Port lintel
7. Internal eyebolt and ring
8. Port sill
9. Blackstrake
10. Wale
11. Pintle of hinge
12. Gudgeon of hinge
13. External planks, conforming to sheer of ship's side planking
14. Hinge brace
15. Eyebolt
16. Ring
17. Plank, conforming to blackstrake
18. Internal planking
19. Joint line of external planks

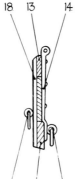

D3/5

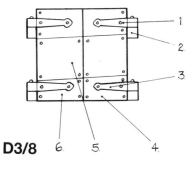

D3/6

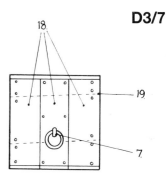

D3/7

D3/8 Foremost port cover (if fitted), external elevation (1/24 scale)

1. Upper hinge brace and gudgeon
2. Hinge pintle
3. Lower hinge brace and gudgeon
4. Right-hand port cover door
5. External planking, conforming to sheer of ship's side planking
6. Left-hand port cover door

This port would be fitted under the forecastle

D3/8

D3/9 Detail of port cover hinge and pintle (1/12 scale)

1. Side elevation of pintle
2. Plan of pintle
3. Pintle (or pin)
4. Securing bolt
5. Plan elevation of hinge brace and gudgeon
6. Side elevation of hinge brace and gudgeon
7. Gudgeon
8. Bolt hole
9. Brace
10. Upset portion of brace to conform to thickness of blackstrake

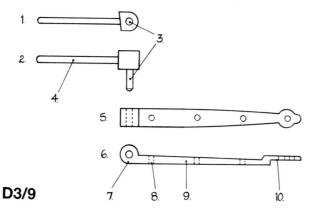

D3/9

D3/10 Sweep port lid (buckler) cross-section and elevation (1/24 scale)

1. Sweep port lintel
2. Sweep port sill
3. Sweep port lid, internal face
4. Eyebolt and ring
5. Sweep port lid, external face
6. Sweep port hinge
7. Sweep port hinge pintle
8. Section view of sweep port lid

D3/10

D3/11 Detail of sweep port hinge and pintle (1/12 scale)

1. Side elevation of hinge
2. Plan of hinge
3. Bolt hole
4. Hinge
5. Gudgeon
6. Pintle
7. Pintle securing bolt
8. Side elevation of pintle
9. Plan of pintle

D3/11

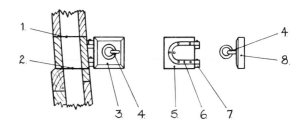

Fittings

E1   **RUDDER AND TILLER (1/48 scale)**

E1/1   **Rudder end view**

E1/2   **Rudder and sternpost side
elevation**

E1/3   **Rudder side elevation, showing
construction**

1. Bolt
2. Mortice for tiller
3. Quarterdeck beam
4. Rudder head
5. Pintle brace
6. Pintle
7. Upper hancing
8. Inner post
9. Gudgeon brace
10. Lower hancing
11. Sternpost
12. Bearding
13. Score
14. Rudder blade
15. Keel
16. Upper false keel (elm)
17. Back piece (fir)
18. Lower false keel (teak)
19. Sole (fir)
20. Bolts
21. Main piece (oak)
22. Fir piece
23. Fir piece

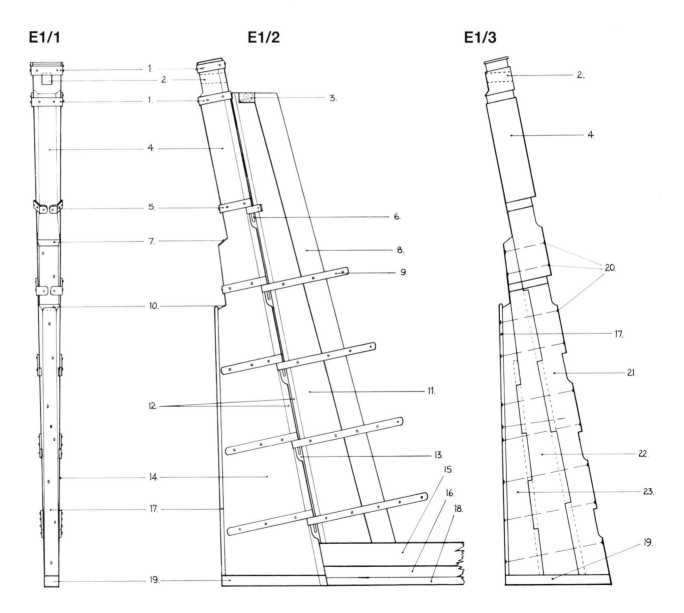

E1/1   **E1/2**   **E1/3**

E Fittings

E1/4

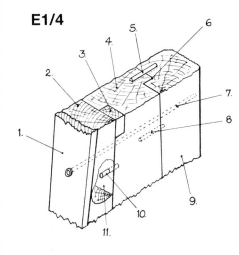

E1/4 Detail of rudder construction (no scale)

1. Back piece
2. After fir piece
3. Section of adjacent timber
4. Fir piece
5. Coak (or dowel)
6. Tabling
7. Clench bolt
8. Coak
9. Main piece
10. Coak (partially shown for clarity)
11. Cutaway for clarity

E1/5 Pintle and gudgeon braces, plan and elevation (1/24 scale)

1. Pintle brace
2. Bolt holes
3. Pintle
4. Copper washer
5. Gudgeon
6. Gudgeon brace
7. Roves
8. Short bolts
9. Rudder timber
10. Brace arm
11. Stern post
12. Inner post
13. Through bolts

E1/5

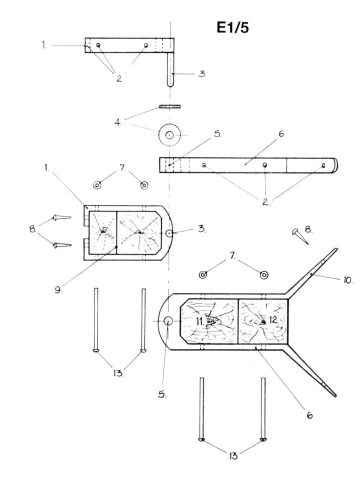

E1/6

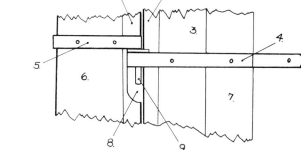

E1/6 Rudder hinge assembly side elevation

1. Bearding of the rudder
2. Bearding of the sternpost
3. Sternpost
4. Gudgeon brace
5. Pintle brace
6. Rudder stock
7. Inner post
8. Score
9. Pintle
10. Copper washer

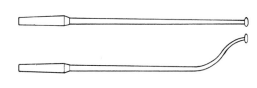

E1/7 Tiller plan and elevation

E1/7

E1/8   Tiller housing plan (1/48 scale)

E1/9   Tiller housing side and forward
        elevations (1/48 scale)

E1/10   Tiller housing isometric projection
        (no scale)

1. Housing canopy
2. Slot for tiller entry
3. Waterway
4. Side panels
5. Tafferal
6. Thickness of panelling
7. Tiller, plan view
8. Tiller, side elevation
9. Tenon to fit into rudder head

E1/8

E1/9

E1/10

E2   PUMPS (1/48 scale)

E2/1   Fore elm tree pump (bilge pump)
        side elevation

E2/2   Fore elm tree pump cross-section
        from aft

1. Brake handle pivot pin
2. Brake handle
3. Hook end of spear (connecting rod)
4. Discharge port
5. Iron hoops
6. Yoke
7. Main hatch ledge
8. Upper deck planking
9. Upper deck beam
10. Pump casing
11. Main mast partners
12. Iron hoops
13. Spear (connecting rod)
14. Pump well cover
15. Reciprocating valve box
16. Pump well support pillar
17. Pump well cross beam
18. Limber board
19. Pump well boarding
20. Fixed valve box (could be withdrawn
    for repair)
21. Pump suction port
22. Keelson
23. Frame
24. Hog
25. Limber strake
26. Keel
27. Limber passage
28. Upper false keel
29. Lower false keel

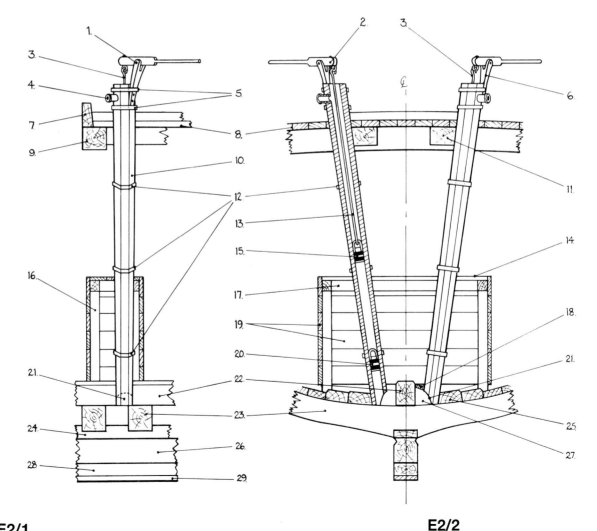
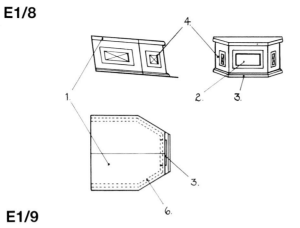
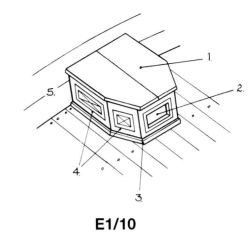

E2/1

E2/2

E Fittings

E2/3 **After elm tree pump (domestic and fire-fighting pump) cross-section from aft**

E2/4 **After elm tree pump side elevation**

E2/5 **After elm tree pump plan**

1. Yoke
2. Hook end of spear (connecting rod)
3. Discharge port
4. Brake handle
5. Iron hoops
6. Pivot pin
7. Pump bore
8. Mizzen mast partners
9. Pump casing head
10. Upper deck beam
11. Pump casing
12. Iron hoops
13. Bore
14. Spear connecting rod
15. Reciprocating valve box
16. After platform deck
17. After platform beam
18. Limber board
19. Fixed valve box (could be withdrawn for repair)
20. Limber strake
21. Frame
22. Keelson
23. Pump sea suction port
24. Limber passage
25. Keel
26. Hog
27. False keels

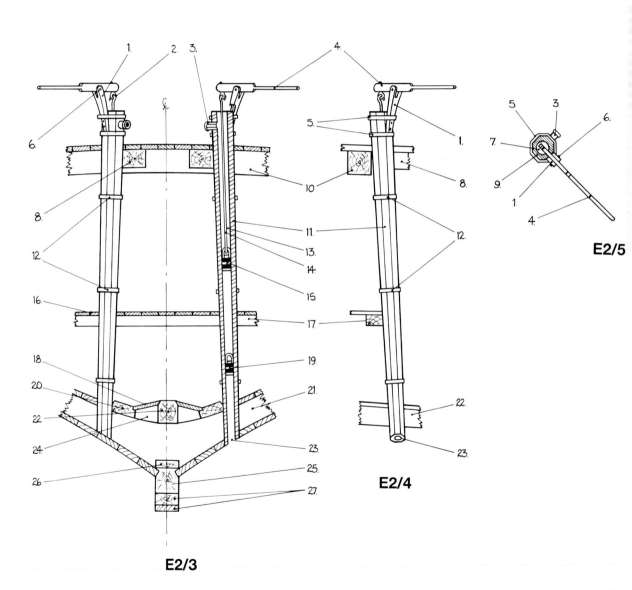

E2/5

E2/4

E2/3

WINDLASS (1/48 scale)

Side elevation

Forward elevation

1. Finger and thumb formed timberhead
2. Belfry support pillar
3. Forelock bolt
4. Cheek (removable)
5. Standard
6. Bolts
7. Windlass spindle
8. Iron strap
9. Upper deck
10. Upper deck beam
11. Carling
12. Heel of the belfry pillar
13. Carrick bitt pin
14. Fore platform deck
15. Platform beam
16. Heel of the bitt pin
17. Removable locking bolt
18. Pawl (iron)
19. Pawl slot
20. Handspike sockets
21. Warping head of spindle
22. Iron hoop
23. Ceiling planks
24. Footwaling
25. Timber (frame)
26. Limberstrake
27. Limber passage
28. Limber board
29. Rising wood
30. Keelson
31. Hog
32. Keel

E3/1

E3/2

77

E Fittings

E3/3 Isometric projection (no scale)

1. Forelock bolt (removable)
2. Handspikes
3. Removable locking bolt
4. Belfry support pillars
5. Bolt hole for handspike
6. Pawl fulcrum bolt
7. Iron pawl
8. Carrick bitt pin
9. Standard
10. Warping head
11. Cheek (removable)
12. Windlass spindle
13. Handspike socket
14. Pawl slot
15. Flat of the upper deck
16. Iron strap
17. Iron hoop

E3/4 Detail of handspike

1. Spindle
2. Handspike sockets
3. Handspike—square in section

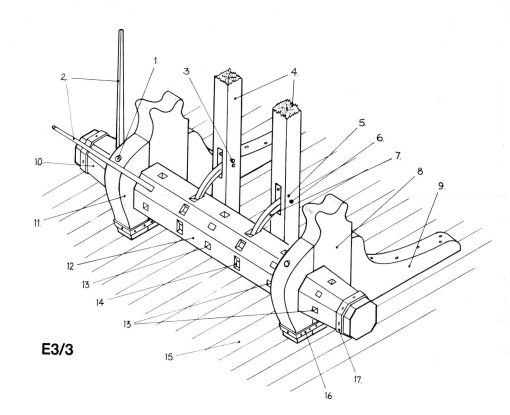

E3/3

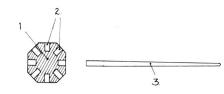

E3/4

E3/5 Detail of pawl arrangements (1/24 scale)

1. Pawl (in disengaged position)
2. Locking bolt (to disengage pawl)
3. Cotter pin for forelock bolt
4. Locking bolt hole
5. Fulcrum bolt for pawl
6. Washer
7. Slot forming pawl housing
8. Iron pawl (in engaged position)
9. Belfry support pillar
10. Pawl slots
11. Spindle

E3/5

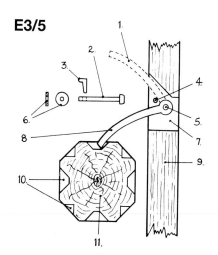

E4/1

E4/2

E4   BELFRY (1/48 scale)

E4/1   After elevation

E4/2   Side elevation

1. Canopy
2. Iron crank for bell rope
3. Headstock pivot bolt
4. Headstock
5. Forecastle planking

6. Bell
7. Forecastle beam
8. Bolts
9. Hole for locking bolt
10. Pawl fulcrum bolt
11. Windlass pawl
12. Locking forelock bolt
13. Belfry support pilar
14. Upper deck planking
15. Upper deck beam
16. Clench bolts

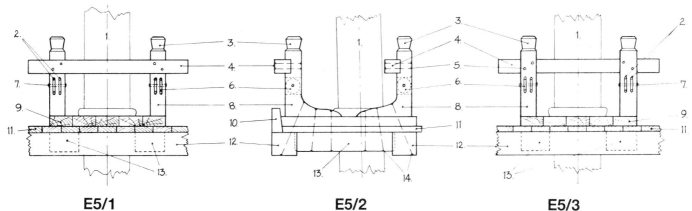

E5/1 **E5/2** **E5/3**

1.	Main mast
2.	Sheave slots
3.	Timberheads
4.	Crosspiece
5.	Clench bolts
6.	Sheave (lignum vitae)
7.	Sheave bolt
8.	Bitt pin (formed into a standard)
9.	Deck reinforcement planking

10.	Main hatch coaming
11.	Upper deck planking
12.	Upper deck beam
13.	Carling, of extra scantling forming mast partners
14.	Clench bolts

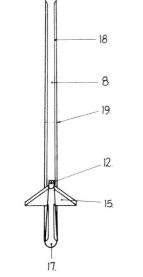

E6/2

E6/1

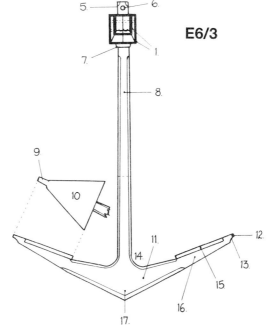

E6/3

1.	Iron bands
2.	Anchor stock (in two parts)
3.	Anchor ring
4.	Timber coaks
5.	Square of the shank
6.	Hole for the anchor ring
7.	Nut (or shoulder)
8.	Shank
9.	Bill
10.	Flat of the palm
11.	Arm
12.	Bill
13.	Snipe
14.	Throat
15.	Palm
16.	Blade
17.	Crown
18.	Chamfered edging
19.	Trend (balance point)

E6/4 **Puddening the anchor ring**

1. Lashing
2. Puddening rope
3. Seizing
4. Anchor ring
5. Shank

E6/5 **Bower anchor with buoy**

1. Buoy
2. Buoy rope
3. Lashings

E6/6 **Kedge anchor, forward elevation**

E6/7 **Kedge anchor, side elevation**

1. Anchor ring
2. Iron stock hoops
3. Eye for the ring
4. Wooden stock
5. Shank
6. Palm
7. Arms
8. Crown

E6/4

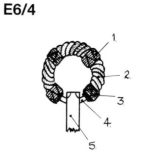

E6/5

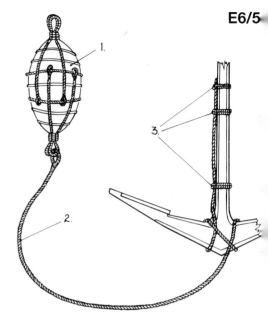

E6/6

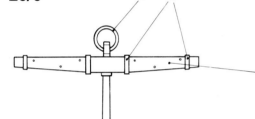

E6/7

E6/8 **Fish davit, plan and elevation**

1. Fish davit, end elevation
2. Handrope eye strops
3. Topping lift eyebolt
4. Fish davit, side elevation
5. Handrope
6. Fish davit, plan
7. Handrope passing to opposite side
8. Necking

E6/9 **Detail of fish davit**

1. Side elevation
2. Plan
3. Hole for handrope eye strop
4. Handrope eye strop

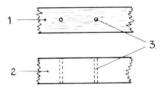

E6/9

E6/8

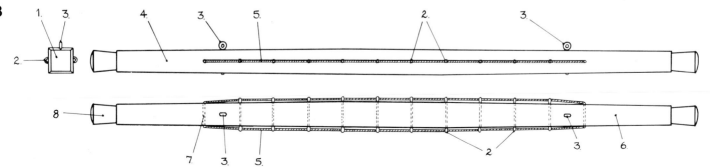

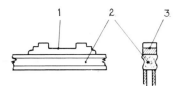

E6/10

E6/10 Detail of fish davit cleat

1. Fish davit cleat
2. Planksheer rail
3. Cross-section of fish davit cleat

E6/11 Detail of spanshackle

1. Spanshackle
2. Spanshackle side view
3. Bolt
4. Spanshackle securing deck eyebolt

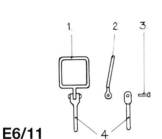

E6/11

E6/12 Manner of rigging the fish davit (rigged to port) (1/96 scale)

1. Fish hook
2. Fish pendant fall
3. Fish tackle block
4. Fish tackle block strop
5. Topping lift eyebolt
6. Fish davit topping lift pendant
7. Pendant block
8. Topping lift tackle
9. Topping lift block
10. Topping lift
11. Fall of the tackle
12. Running part of fish pendant
13. Fish pendant block
14. Standing part of fish pendant tackle
15. Running part of fish pendant tackle
16. Spanshackle
17. Carling through which spanshackle deck eyebolt is secured
18. Fish davit
19. Upper deck beam
20. Deck planking
21. Spanshackle (not in use) employed when davit rigged to starboard
22. Bulwark with fist davit cleat on planksheer rail

E6/13 Cathead plan (starboard) (1/48 scale)

E6/14 Cathead side elevation from aft

E6/15 Cathead sheave slot cross-section

1. Sheave slot
2. Sheave
3. Sheave pin
4. Cathead, inboard end
5. Planksheer
6. Outboard cap
7. Carving details of cap: lion's (cat's) head
8. Forecastle deck beams
9. Bolts
10. Cleat for cathead stopper
11. Forecastle deck
12. Frame
13. Panel ornamentation

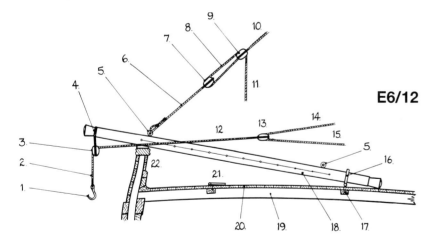

E6/12

E6/15

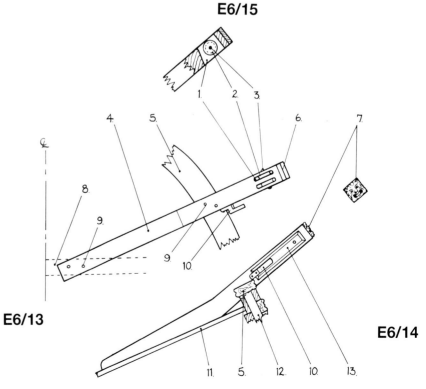

E6/13

E6/14

E6/16

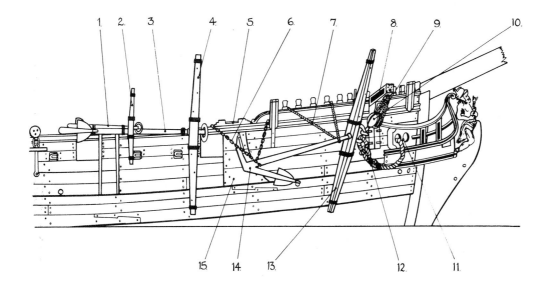

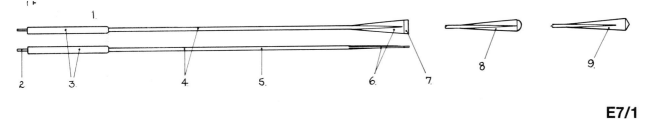

E7/1

E8   GALLEY FIREHEARTH AND KETTLE (1/48 scale)

E8/1   Side elevation

E8/2   Longitudinal cross-section

E8/3   Elevation from aft

1. Flue cover
2. Guide spigot
3. Cover guide
4. Flue hood
5. Cowling
6. Housing
7. Forecastle deck
8. Forecastle beam
9. Joint seam
10. Flue uptake
11. Housing
12. Upper deck
13. Upper deck beam
14. Hook
15. Smoke flap
16. Grate bars
17. Ash tray
18. Fore platform deck
19. Platform beam
20. Stanchions
21. Carling
22. Fore bulkhead
23. Oven door
24. Nozzle and drain cock
25. Heat duct door
26. Firehearth side brickwork
27. Division brickwork
28. Baffle
29. Kettle lid
30. Firehearth grate
31. Oven grill bars
32. Oven division wall
33. Heat duct to oven
34. Baffle (partially omitted for clarity)
35. Kettle support bars (iron)
36. Heat outlet ducts to flue
37. Copper kettle
38. Oven door hinges
39. Hinges

All fittings for the firehearth, ovens and flue uptakes are made of iron; all fittings for the kettles are of copper. The drain cocks are made of brass

E8/4   Copper kettle end elevation and cross-section

1. Lid handle
2. Kettle lid
3. Joint seams
4. Drain joint seam
5. Rivet
6. Seam overlap
7. Nozzle
8. Drain cock handle
9. Drain cock valve

E8/5   Details of firehearth

1. Iron hood
2. Oven door hinge
3. Heat duct door (iron)
4. Heat duct (door omitted for clarity)
5. Oven door (iron)
6. Drain cock
7. Heat outlet duct
8. Baffle (iron)
9. Top edge of baffle
10. Flue uptake

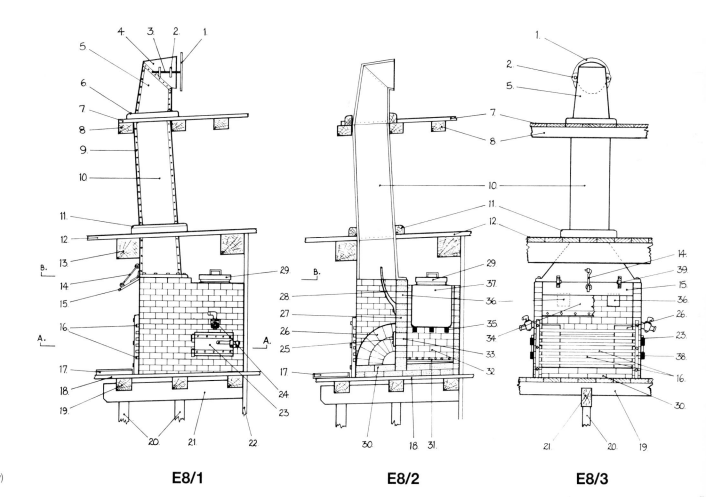

E8/1   **E8/2**   **E8/3**

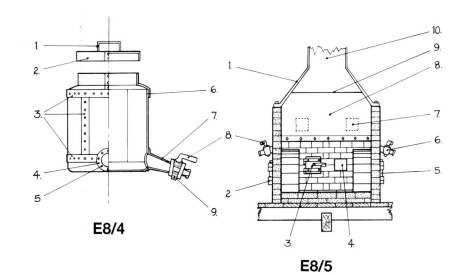

E8/4   **E8/5**

E Fittings

E8/6 **Firehearth and kettle cross-section at top**

E8/7 **Cross-section at middle level**

E8/8 **Cross-section below flue**

1. Flue uptake
2. Hood
3. Square-headed bolts
4. Closure brickwork
5. Kettle lid
6. Drain cock
7. Side brickwork
8. Transverse brickwork
9. Heat duct (partly open position)
10. Sub-division brickwork
11. Fire hearth side brickwork
12. Grate bar support
13. Grate bar
14. Side brickwork
15. Heat duct
16. Division brickwork
17. Oven door (iron)
18. Transverse oven grill bars
19. Fore and aft oven grill bars
20. Heat duct door (in closed position)
21. Grate
22. Baffle
23. Copper kettle

E9 **MESS TABLE AND STOOLS (1/48 scale)**

E9/1 **Plan and elevation**

E9/2 **Isometric projection (no scale)**

1. Table top
2. Holes for hanging strop
3. Hooks for securing to ship's side
4. Stool
5. Bracket
6. Hanging strop hooked to beam
7. Hooks set into eyebolts

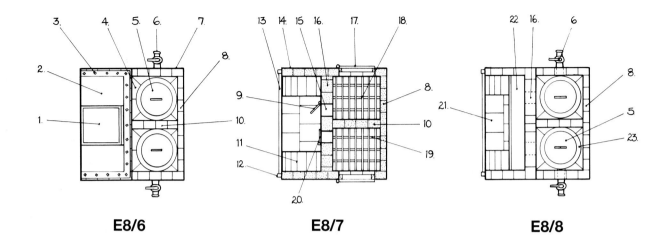

E8/6   **E8/7**   **E8/8**

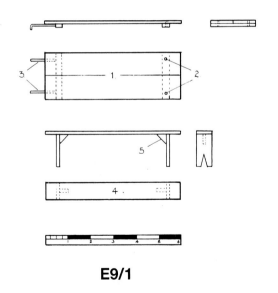

E9/1

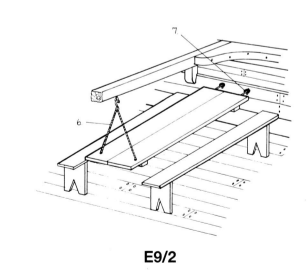

E9/2

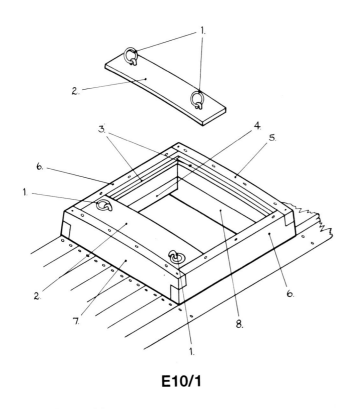

E10/1

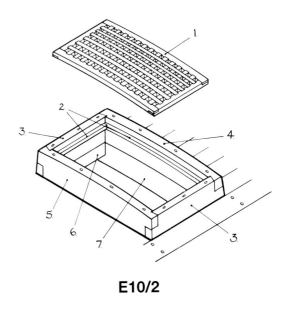

E10/2

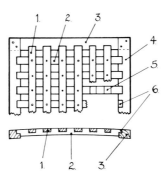

E10/3

E10   HATCHES AND GRATINGS

**E10/1 Main hatchway isometric
         projection (no scale)**

1. Lifting rings
2. Hatch cover board (4 in number) 2in
    thick
3. Battens
4. Carling
5. Fore head ledge
6. Coaming
7. After head ledge
8. Upper deck beam

**E10/2 Fore hatchway isometric
         projection (no scale)**

1. Grating
2. Battens
3. Coaming
4. Fore head ledge
5. After head ledge
6. Carling
7. Upper deck beam

E10/3 Detail of grating (1/24 scale)

1. Athwartships batten (2 × 1in)
2. Cross batten (2 × 2in)
3. Edging frame (3 × 2½ × 1in)
4. Athwartships edging frame (3 × 2½
    × 1in)
5. Recess in cross batten (2 × 1in)
6. Recess in edging frame (1 × 1in)

F Armament

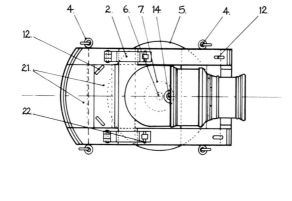

F1/1

F1/2

F1/3

F1/4

F1/5

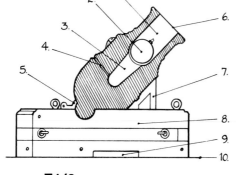

F1/6

An alternative, later method of supporting the mortar in the firing position – by the use of a wooden chock – is illustrated in Photograph 15.

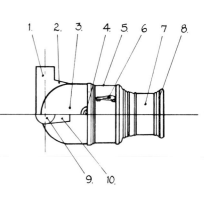

F1/7

F2   10IN MORTAR AND BED (1/48 scale)

F2/1   Side elevation of mortar and bed

F2/2   Front elevation of mortar and bed

F2/3   Plan of bed

F2/4   Side elevation of mortar

F2/5   Plan of mortar

1.   Bed lifting eyebolt
2.   Cap square
3.   Trunnion
4.   Cap square retaining bolt
5.   Bed cheek
6.   Mortar
7.   Dolphins
8.   Cotter pin to retain cap square
9.   Transom piece
10.   Bed base
11.   Turntable
12.   Traversing ring and eyebolt
13.   Iron spindle
14.   Turntable, set into bed base
15.   Traversing ring and eyebolt
16.   10in shell
17.   Upper timber block
18.   Timber block, middle tier
19.   Cap square hinge and bolt
20.   Bed base timbers
21.   Web to strengthen trunnions
22.   Vent
23.   Charge chamber
24.   Shell chamber
25.   Breech
26.   Vent and pan
27.   Royal monogram

F2/1

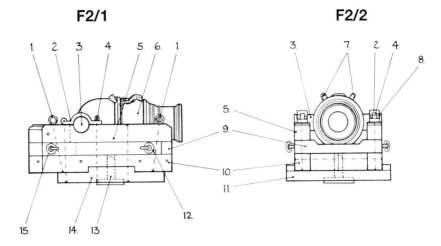

F2/2

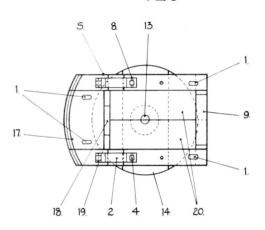

F2/3

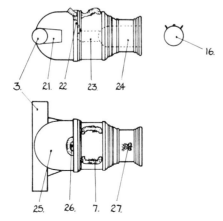

F2/4

F2/5

F Armament

F3 **10IN HOWITZER (1/48 scale)**

F3/1 **Rear elevation of bed assembly**

F3/2 **Side elevation of howitzer and bed**

F3/3 **Front elevation of bed assembly**

F3/4 **Detail of quoin**

F3/5 **Plan of howitzer and bed**

F3/5 **Plan of howitzer**

F3/7 **Underneath plan of bed assembly**

F3/8 **Cross-section of bed assembly**

1. Cap square bolt
2. Iron cap square
3. Bed cheek
4. Vertical bolts
5. Trunnion
6. Howitzer
7. Ring bolt
8. Bed base (two pieces)
9. Quoin
10. Transverse bolts
11. Transom
12. Slot for retaining key
13. Iron spindle
14. Turntable
15. Hand groove
16. Side elevation of quoin
17. Plan elevation of quoin
18. Shell
19. Raised section of turntable
20. Cap square retaining pin
21. Cascable
22. Vent and pan
23. Charge chamber
24. Shell chamber
25. Ring bolt fastening

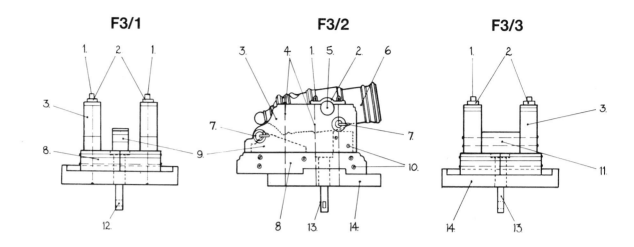

F3/1   F3/2   F3/3

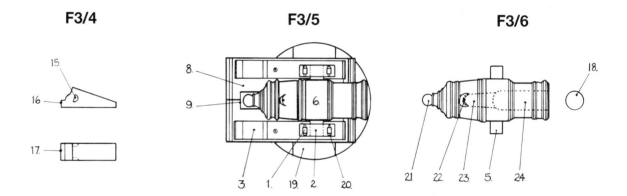

F3/4   F3/5   F3/6

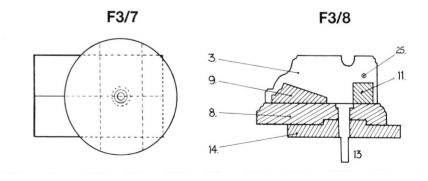

F3/7   F3/8

F4 **SHELLS, FUSES AND CARCASSES**

F4/1 Cross-section of 13in shell (1/16 scale)

F4/2 Detail of beechwood fuse (1/4 scale)

F4/3 Side elevation of a carcass cage (1/16 scale)

F4/4 External view of a 13in shell (1/16 scale)

F4/5 Cross-section of a 10in shell (1/16 scale)

F4/6 Mortar shell (10 and 13in) (no scale)

F4/7 Carcass (no scale)

1. Lifting lug
2. Fuse hole
3. Cavity for charge
4. Shell case wall
5. Shell case
6. Beechwood fuse
7. Pitch sealing, removed when required
8. Cross-section of fuse
9. External view of fuse
10. Timing divisions
11. Lifting lugs
12. Vent holes
13. Upper case
14. Vertical iron cage pieces
15. Horizontal iron cage pieces
16. Rivets
17. Lower case
18. Cavity for combustibles

F4/1

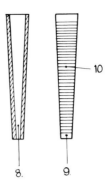

F4/2

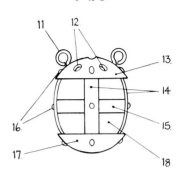

F4/3

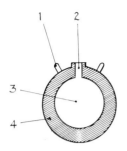

F4/4

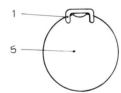

F4/5

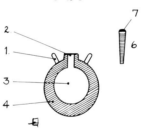

F4/6

F4/7

89

F5 **4-POUNDER CARRIAGE GUN**
(1/24 scale)

F5/1 Rear elevation of carriage
assembly

F5/2 Side elevation of carriage (trucks
omitted for clarity)

F5/3 Side elevation of carriage and gun

F5/4 Plan of carriage

F5/5 Side elevation of gun

F5/6 Plan of gun

F5/7 Detail of royal monogram of
George II, c1740 (no scale)

F5/8 Cross-section of 4-pounder
breech, showing charge and shot

1.	Axle pin
2.	Front truck
3.	Eye bolt and ring
4.	Cap square
5.	Transom
6.	Quoin
7.	Carriage cheek
8.	Rear axletree
9.	Bolster (or pig)
10.	Rear ringbolt
11.	Bed
12.	Rear truck
13.	Ringbolt
14.	Cap square bolt
15.	Cap square retaining bolt
16.	Transverse bolt
17.	Front ringbolt
18.	Front axletree
19.	Iron bracket
20.	Tie bolt
21.	Hole for axle pin
22.	Cascable
23.	Vent and pan
24.	Trunnion
25.	Chain
26.	Cotter pin to retain cap square
27.	Dowel joining truck halves together
28.	Base ring
29.	Vent
30.	Bore
31.	Face
32.	Breech
33.	Vent field
34.	First reinforce
35.	Second reinforce
36.	Chase
37.	Muzzle
38.	Swell
39.	4lb shot, 3½in diameter
40.	Cartridge containing charge
41.	Wooden wad

F5/1   **F5/2**   **F5/3**

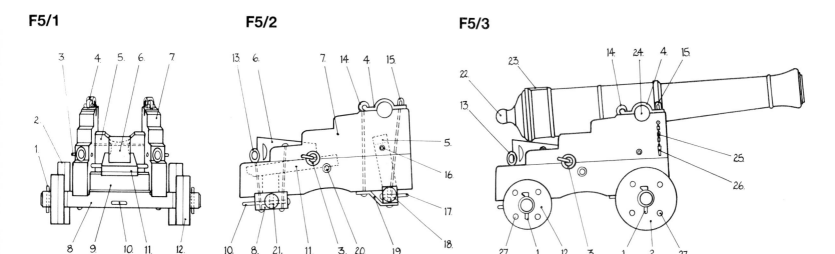

F5/5   **F5/7**

F5/4   **F5/6**   **F5/8**

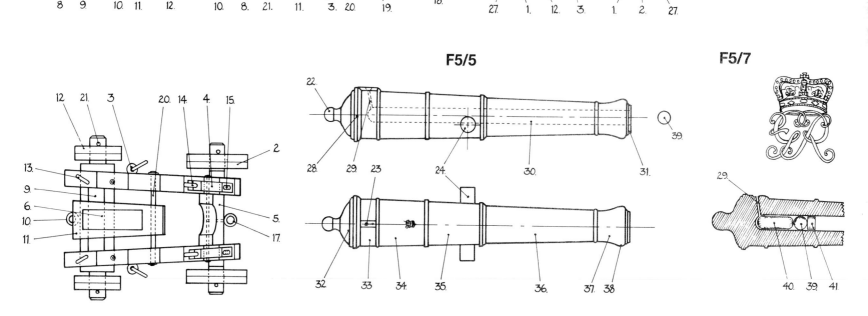

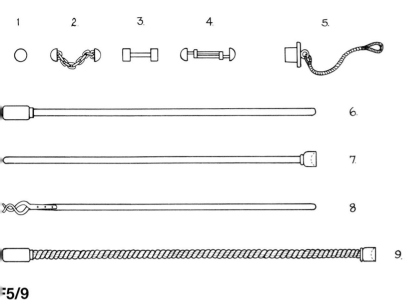

F5/9

F5/9 Shot and equipment for 4-pounder gun

1. Solid round shot
2. Chain shot
3. Bar shot
4. Expanding shot
5. Tampion and lanyard
6. Sponge
7. Ram rod
8. Worm
9. Flexible rammer and sponge combined

F5/10 Gun tackle elevation

F5/11 Gun tackle plan

1. Gun tackle fall
2. Traversing tackle fall
3. Gunport
4. Eyebolt
5. Eyebolt and ring
6. 3in single block
7. Traversing tackle
8. 3in double block
9. Breeching
10. 4in single block
11. Gun tackle
12. 4in double block
13. Eyebolt and ring

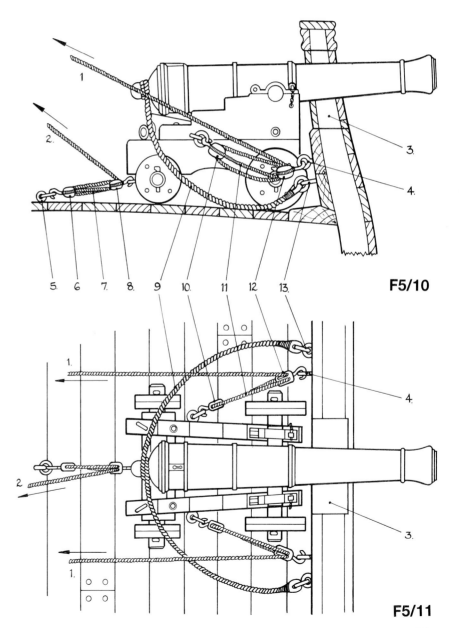

F5/10

F5/11

F Armament

F6   **HALF-POUNDER SWIVEL GUN**

F6/1   **Pedestal and railing, side elevation (1/48 scale)**

F6/2   **Swivel gun, pedestal and railing, end elevation (1/48 scale)**

1.   Iron hoop (½in thick)
2.   Socket to receive swivel pintle
3.   Swivel gun in mounted position
4.   Swivel mounting (or yoke)
5.   Rough tree rail (fife rail if associated with the forecastle)
6.   Gun pedestal
7.   Planksheer rail
8.   Quarterdeck (this may also represent the forecastle)
9.   Ship's side

F6/3   **Profile of gun and swivel mounting**

F6/3   **Profile of gun and swivel mounting (1/24 scale)**

F6/4   **Swivel mounting, end elevation**

F6/5   **Swivel gun, plan (mounting omitted)**

1.   Cascable, formed as a training handle
2.   Flash pan and vent
3.   Bore
4.   Trunnion
5.   End elevation of muzzle
6.   Retaining bushes
7.   Swivel mounting pintle
8.   Half-pound solid shot

F6/1   **F6/2**

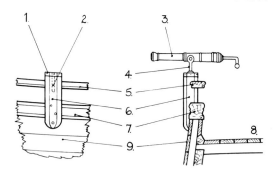

F6/3   **F6/4**

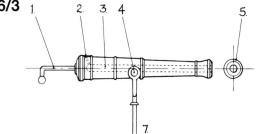
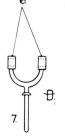

F6/5

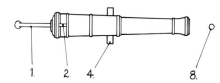

G Masts and yards

1

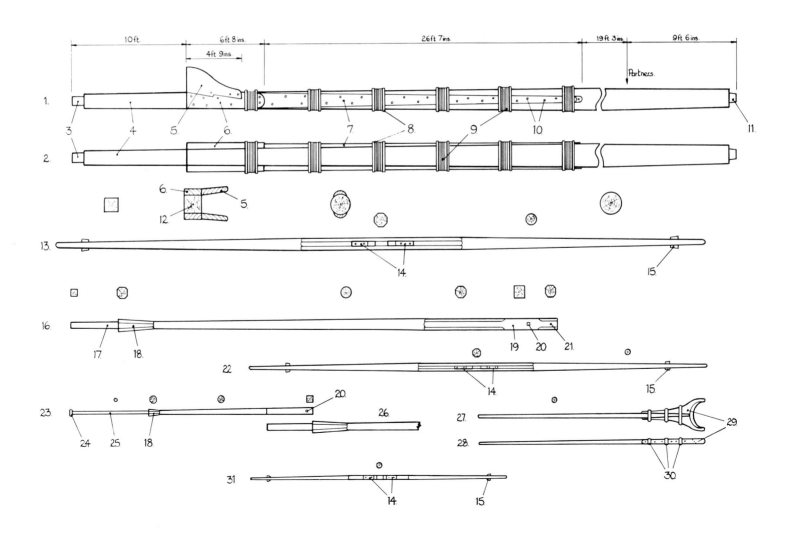

G2   **MIZZEN MASTS, YARDS AND BOOMS (1/96 scale)**

1. Mizzen lower mast (side view)
2. Lower mast head (fore and aft view)
3. Lower mast head
4. Cheeks
5. Coaks
6. Heel tenon
7. Tenon for mast cap
8. Cheeks (end view)
9. Crossjack yard
10. Sling cleats
11. Yard arm cleats
12. Mizzen topmast
13. Topmast head
14. Sheave
15. Hole for fid
16. Heel
17. Mizzen topgallant mast
18. Mast truck
19. Square section of topgallant mast
20. Hole for fid
21. Topsail yard
22. Combined topmast and topgallant mast (employed as an alternative to 12)
23. Polehead topgallant mast
24. Rigging stop
25. Topgallant yard
26. Gaff
27. Iron retention bands
28. Jaws
29. Boom
30. Boom end cleats

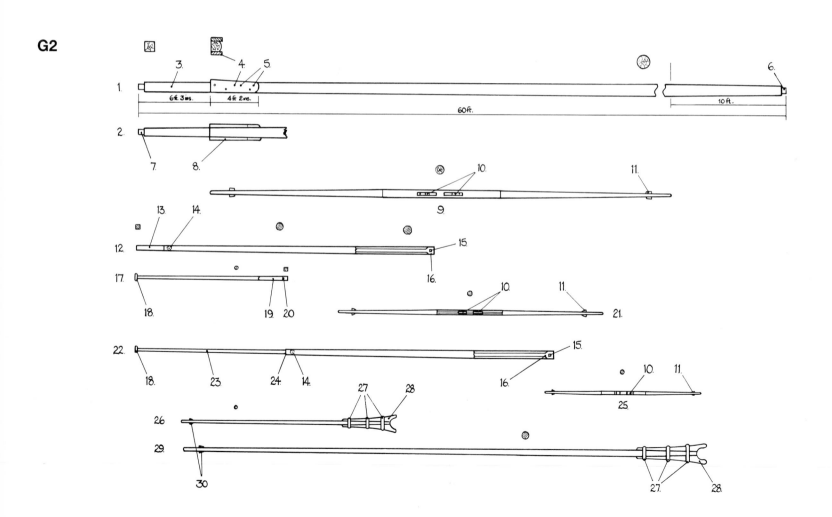

G2

G3 **BOWSPRIT, JIBBOOM AND YARD**
(1/96 scale)

1.   Bowsprit (side view)
2.   Bowsprit (plan view)
3.   Heel tenon
4.   Position of the bed
5.   Gammon cleats
6.   Woolding
7.   Spritsail yard saddle
8.   Woolding hoops
9.   Jibboom heel chock
10. Square section of bowsprit head
11. Tenon for mast cap
12. Jibboom (side view)
13. Jibboom (plan view)
14. Jibboom heel and tenon
15. Sheave
16. Sheave slot
17. Rigging stop
18. Spritsail yard
19. Sling cleats
20. Yard arm cleats

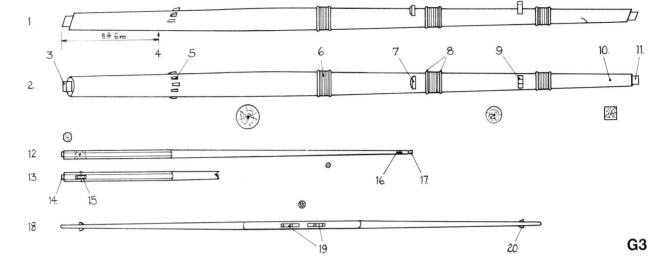

G3

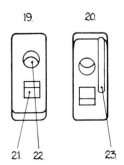

G4/1

G4/2

G4 **DETAIL OF THE BOWSPRIT HEAD**
(1/48 scale)

G4/1 Cross-section at jibboom heel chock

G4/2 Side elevation of bowsprit head

G4/3 Plan elevation of bowsprit head

G4/4 Detail of the bowsprit cap

1.   Jibboom heel chock
2.   Cross-section of bowsprit
3.   Jibboom heel retaining pin
4.   Rope slot
5.   Sheave and pin
6.   Sheave slot
7.   Jibboom heel
8.   Seating of the bees
9.   Bowsprit (round section)
10. Woolding hoop
11. Woolding
12. Square section head of bowsprit
13. Bee block
14. Sheave
15. Hole for emergency topmast stay
16. Bowsprit cap
17. Hole for jibboom heel retaining pin
18. Sheave slot for main topmast stay
19. Front elevation of cap
20. After side of cap
21. Mortice for bowsprit head tenon
22. Hole for jibboom
23. Slot for jackstaff

G4/3

G4/4

G Masts and yards

G5 **DETAIL OF THE MAIN MAST HEAD, CAP, TRESTLETREES, CROSSTREES AND MAIN TOP** (1/96 scale)

G5/1 Side elevation

G5/2 Front elevation

G5/3 Plan elevation of trestletrees and crosstrees

G5/4 Plan elevation of main top

1. Plan view of cap
2. Mast head hoop
3. Cap
4. Mast head batten
5. Main top mast
6. Top rail
7. Mast head cleat
8. Bolster
9. Rail stanchions
10. Outer rim
11. Top planking
12. Crosstrees
13. Trestletrees
14. Bibs
15. Woolding
16. Topmast heel
17. Gunwale
18. Mortice for top rail stanchions
19. Mortice for futtock shrouds and topmast shroud deadeye plates
20. Aftermast top planking
21. Fore and aft planking
22. Side rim
23. Foremost top timber
24. Holes for crowsfeet
25. Main mast head
26. Lubber piece of crosstree
27. Battens
28. Fore rim
29. Iron plate for fid
30. Iron fid

G5/1

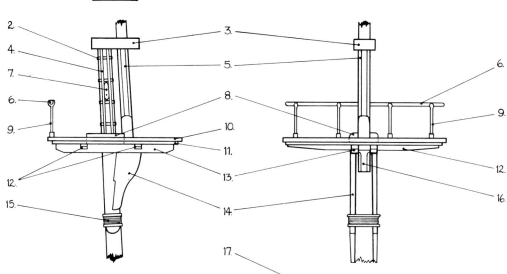

G5/2

G5/3

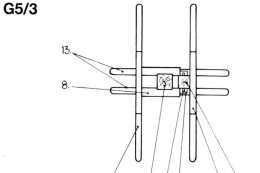

G5/4

G5/5

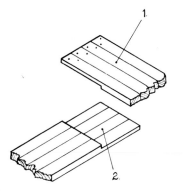

G5/5 Detail of top planking overlap joints (1/24 scale)

1. Athwartships planking
2. Fore and aft planking

G6/1

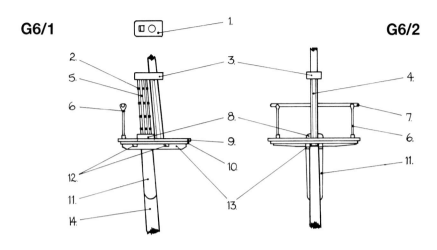

1.
2.
5.
6.
8.
9.
10.
12.
11.
13.
14.

G6/2

3.
4.
7.
6.
11.
13.

G6/3

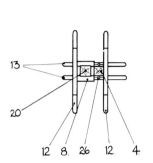

13
20
12 8 26 12 4

G6   DETAIL OF THE MIZZEN MAST HEAD, CAP, TRESTLETREES, CROSSTREES AND MIZZEN TOP (1/96 scale)

G6/1   Side elevation

G6/2   Front elevation

G6/3   Plan elevation of trestletrees and crosstrees

G6/4   Plan elevation of mizzen top

1.   Mizzen mast cap (plan view)
2.   Mast head hoops
3.   Mast head cap
4.   Mizzen topmast
5.   Mast head battens
6.   Top rail stanchion
7.   Top rail
8.   Bolster
9.   Outer rim
10. Top planking
11. Cheek
12. Crosstrees
13. Trestletrees
14. Mizzen mast
15. Mortice for top rail stanchions
16. Gunwale
17. Fore and aft top planking
18. Side rim
19. Mortice for futtock shrouds and mizzen topmast shroud deadeye plates
20. Mizzen mast head
21. The fore rim
22. The outer rim
23. Battens
24. Holes for crowsfeet
25. Foremost top planking
26. Fid and iron plate

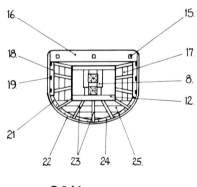

16.
18.
19.
21
22 23 24 25.
15.
17.
8.
12.

G6/4

G7   DETAIL OF MAST WOOLDING (1/24 scale)

1.   Woolding hoop
2.   Woolding
3.   Mast

This applies to all woolded masts

G7

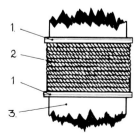

1.
2.
1
3.

G Masts and yards

G8   MAIN TOPMAST HEAD (1/48 scale)

G8/1 Side elevation

G8/2 Front elevation

G8/3 Plan of trestletrees and crosstrees

G8/4 Detail of main topmast cap

1.   Main topgallant mast
2.   Main topmast cap
3.   Main topmast head
4.   Bolster
5.   Fid (iron)
6.   Trestletrees
7.   Crosstrees
8.   Topmast hounds
9.   Main topmast
10. Holes for the topgallant shrouds
11. Iron fid plate
12. Mortice for topmast head
13. Hole for topgallant mast

G9   MIZZEN TOPMAST HEAD (1/48 scale)

G9/1 Detail of mizzen topmast cap

G9/2 Side elevation

G9/3 Front elevation

G9/4 Plan of trestletrees and crosstrees

1.   Mizzen topmast cap
2.   Mizzen topgallant mast
3.   Mizzen topmast head
4.   Fid (iron)
5.   Bolster
6.   Trestletrees
7.   Crosstrees
8.   Mizzen topmast
9.   Holes for mizzen topgallant shrouds
10. Iron fid plate

G8/1

G8/2

G8/3

G8/4

G9/1

G9/2

G9/3

G9/4

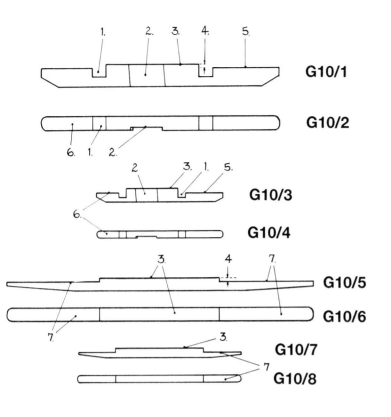

G10/1

G10/2

G10/3

G10/4

G10/5

G10/6

G10/7

G10/8

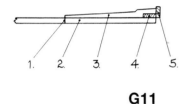

G11

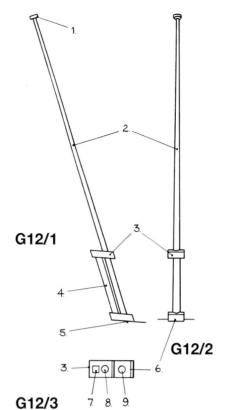

G12/1

G12/2

G12/3

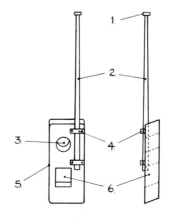

G13/1

G13/2

G10 **DETAIL OF TRESTLETREES AND CROSSTREES (1/48 scale)**

G10/1 Inboard elevation of main trestletree

G10/2 Plan of main trestletree

G10/3 Inboard elevation of mizzen trestletree

G10/4 Plan of mizzen trestletree

G10/5 Side elevation of main crosstree

G10/6 Plan of main crosstree

G10/7 Side elevation of mizzen crosstree

G10/8 Plan of mizzen crosstree

1. Score to receive crosstree
2. Score to fit mast head
3. Lubber wood
4. Height of lubber wood (thickness of top planking — additional to trestletree or crosstree depth)
5. Land for foremost top planking
6. Land for aftermost top planking
7. Land for side planking

G11 **CROSS-SECTION OF TOP (1/48 scale)**

1. Boundary of square hole of top
2. Top planking
3. Batten
4. Rim
5. Outer rim

G12 **ENSIGN STAFF AND TABERNACLE (1/48 scale)**

G12/1 Side elevation

G12/2 End elevation from forward

G12/3 Plan of tabernacle

1. Truck
2. Ensign staff
3. Staff cap
4. Stiffener
5. Line depicts top surface of rudder head housing
6. Shoe
7. Mortice for stiffener (identical on shoe)
8. Hole for staff
9. Circular recess for ensign staff heel

G13 **JACKSTAFF AND HOUSING (1/48 scale)**

G13/1 End elevation from aft

G13/2 Side elevation

1. Truck
2. Jackstaff
3. Hole for jibboom
4. Iron retaining brackets
5. Bowsprit cap
6. Mortice for bowsprit head tenon

H1

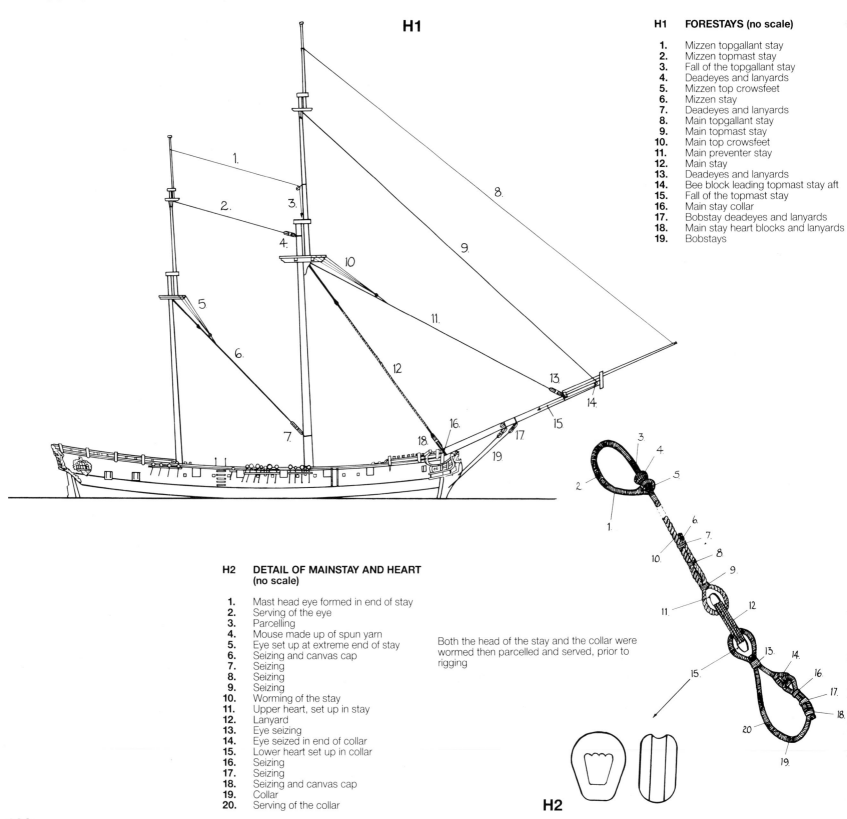

Both the head of the stay and the collar were wormed then parcelled and served, prior to rigging

H2

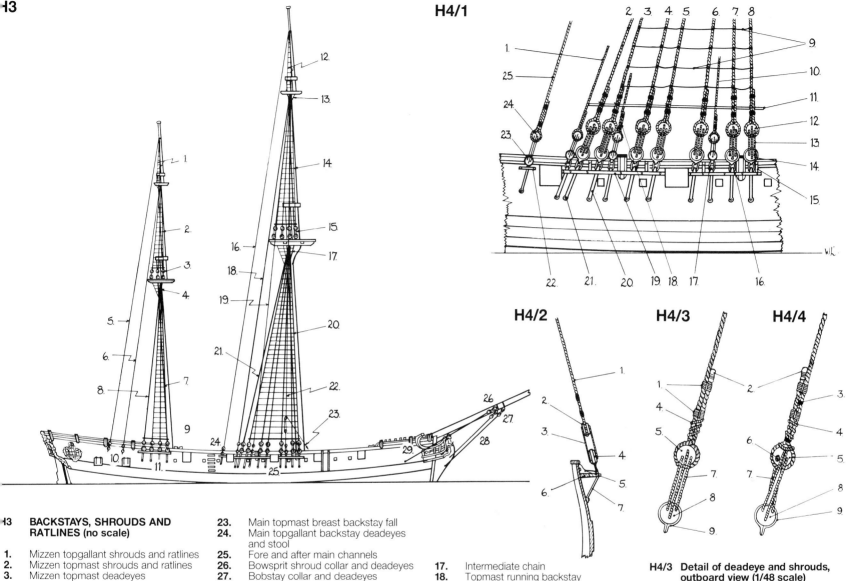

H3

H4/1

H4/2　H4/3　H4/4

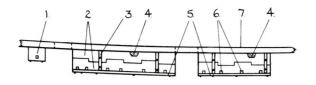

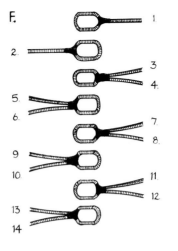

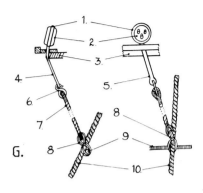

H4/5

H4/6

H4/7

H4/5 Main channel, plan view (1/96 scale)

1. Main topgallant standing backstay stool
2. Channel boards (tabled together)
3. Channel knee (standard)
4. Swivel gun stanchion
5. Channel retaining paunch
6. Chain plate slots
7. Ship's side

H4/6 Order of laying shrouds over the mast head (no scale)

1. Larboard 7th shroud
2. Starboard 7th shroud
3. Larboard 6th shroud
4. Starboard 6th shroud
5. Larboard 5th shroud
6. Starboard 5th shroud
7. Larboard 4th shroud
8. Starboard 4th shroud
9. Larboard 3rd shroud
10. Starboard 3rd shroud
11. Larboard 2nd shroud
12. Starboard 2nd shroud
13. Larboard 1st shroud
14. Starboard 1st shroud

H4/7 Detail of futtock shroud, section and side elevation (no scale)

1. Chain plate strop
2. Lower topmast deadeye
3. Main top
4. Chain plate—end elevation
5. Chain plate—side elevation
6. Futtock shroud
7. Lashing
8. Futtock stave
9. Lower shroud

H5 GAMMON LASHING (no scale)

1. Bowsprit
2. Gammon cleats
3. Gammon lashing
4. Centre lashing (made from tail end of lashing, seized in place)
5. Knee of the head
6. Slot for gammon lashing
7. Lower cheek
8. Trailboard
9. Upper cheek and hair bracket
10. Hole for main stay collar
11. Line of the top surface of the bowsprit
12. Line of the upper edge of the gammon slot
13. Eye spliced into one end of gammon lashing

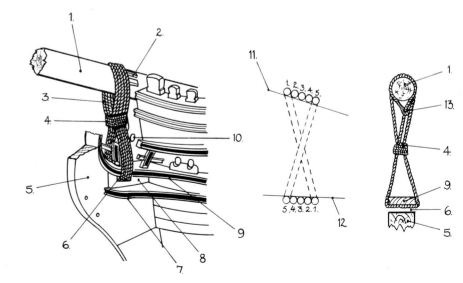

H5

1. Topgallant brace block and pendant
2. Topgallant sail
3. Topgallant bowline and bridle
4. Topgallant sheet block and sheet
5. Standing part of topgallant brace
6. Topsail brace block and pendant
7. Running part of topgallant brace
8. Topgallant bowline lead blocks
9. Topsail
10. Topgallant brace fall block (two; one omitted for clarity)
11. Topgallant brace falls
12. Topgallant sheet fall
13. Standing part of topsail brace
14. Running part of topsail brace
15. Topsail bowline and bridles
16. Bowline lead blocks
17. Topgallant stay
18. Topsail sheet block and sheet
19. Topsail brace fall block (two; one omitted for clarity)
20. Main brace block and pendant
21. Topmast stay
22. Main sail
23. Topsail brace falls
24. Mizzen stay
25. Running part of main brace
26. Topgallant bowline lead fall
27. Topsail bowline lead fall
28. Main bowline and bridles
29. Topsail sheet fall
30. Main bowline lead fall
31. Standing part of main brace
32. Running part of main sheet
33. Standing part of main sheet
34. Main course tack

Larboard side main brace omitted for clarity

H6

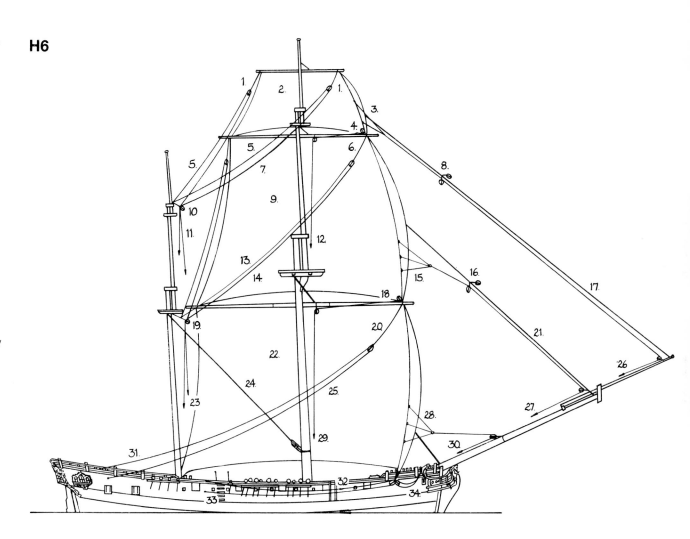

H7 **RUNNING RIGGING OF THE MAIN COURSE (fore side of sail to left, after side to right; 1/96 scale)**

1. Buntline fall block
2. Buntline falls
3. Mainmast shroud
4. Dashed line shows futtock shrouds
5. Yard tackle pendant tricing line
6. Main course reef tackle
7. Standing clew line block
8. Yard tackle pendant tricing line block
9. Running part of the topsail sheet
10. Buntline blocks
11. Yard tackle tricing line fall block
12. Topsail sheet fall block
13. Stirrup
14. Reef tackle lead blocks
15. Foot rope
16. Yard tackle running block
17. Yard tackle and falls
18. Yard tackle standing block
19. Yard tackle pendant
20. Main brace block and pendant
21. Tricing line fall
22. Topsail sheet fall
23. Buntlines
24. Running part of clewline
25. Standing part of clewline
26. Clewline fall
27. Ticked line denotes main shroud
28. Bowline and bridles
29. Clew block
30. Main course sheet block
31. Main course sheets
32. Main course tack

H7

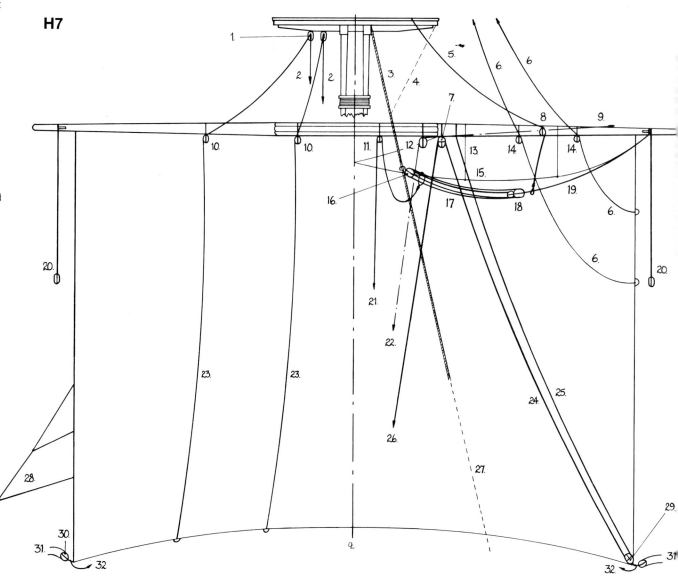

48 **RUNNING RIGGING OF THE MAIN TOPSAIL** (fore side of sail on left, after side to right; 1/96 scale)

1. Buntline fall (directed upward for clarity)
2. Buntline fall block, seized to tie block
3. Standing part of reef tackle, seized to mast head
4. Reef tackle standing block, seized to shrouds (sometimes a sister block)
5. Running part of reef tackle
6. Yardarm sheave for reef tackle pendant
7. Main topsail yard
8. Main topgallant sheet fall block
9. Stirrup
10. Foot rope
11. Standing clewline block
12. Reef tackle pendant
13. Topsail yard brace and pendant
14. Topgallant sheet fall
15. Running part of clewline
16. Standing part of clewline
17. Reef tackle fall
18. Buntline
19. Main topmast shroud
20. Clewline fall
21. Bridles
22. Bowline
23. Main topsail sheet
24. Sheet block
25. Main yard lift block
26. Topsail sheet
27. Main yard
28. Main topsail sheet fall block

H8

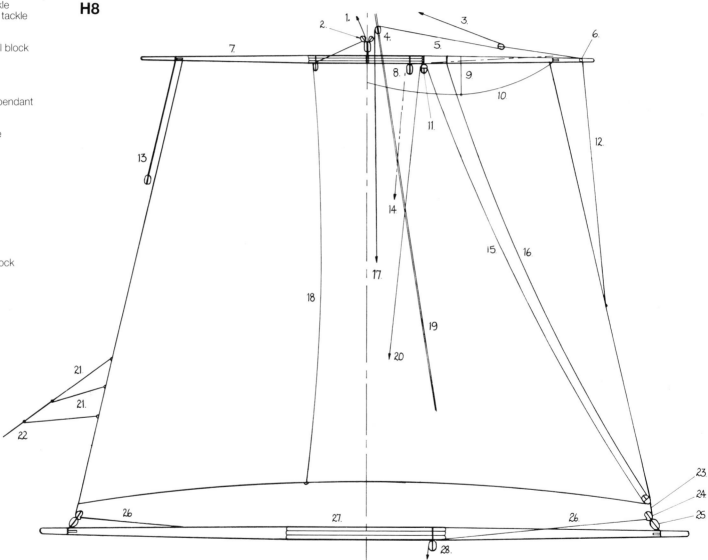

105

H9 **RUNNING RIGGING OF THE MAIN TOPGALLANT SAIL (fore side of sail to left, after side to right; 1/96 scale)**

1. Topgallant yard lift block
2. Lift (standing part seized to mast)
3. Reef tackle standing block (seized to mast)
4. Reef tackle
5. Yardarm sheave for reef tackle pendant
6. Lift fall block (seized to mast)
7. Topgallant yard
8. Footrope
9. Reef tackle pendant
10. Standing clewline block
11. Topgallant brace block and pendant
12. Lift fall
13. Reef tackle fall
14. Clewline fall
15. Bowline and bridle
16. Running part of clewline
17. Standing part of clewline
18. Clew block
19. Sheet block
20. Topsail yard lift block
21. Topgallant sheet
22. Topsail yard
23. Standing sheet block
24. Topgallant sheet fall

H10 **RUNNING RIGGING OF THE MIZZEN MAST (no scale)**

1. Topgallant brace pendant
2. Main topgallant mast backstay
3. Topgallant brace (partially omitted for clarity)
4. Topgallant brace
5. Topgallant sail bridle and bowline
6. Topgallant sheet and fall
7. Topsail brace pendant
8. Topgallant bowline fall
9. Topsail brace (partially omitted for clarity)
10. Standing part of brace
11. Running part of topsail brace
12. Standing part of topgallant brace
13. Topsail bridle and bowlines
14. Peak blocks for topsail and topgallant braces
15. Topsail bowline fall
16. Topsail sheet
17. Crossjack brace, leading to starboard main topmast backstay
18. Crossjack brace, leading to port main topmast backstay
19. Fall of topgallant brace
20. Fall of topsail sheet
21. Fall of crossjack brace
22. Fall of topsail brace
23. Main topmast backstay

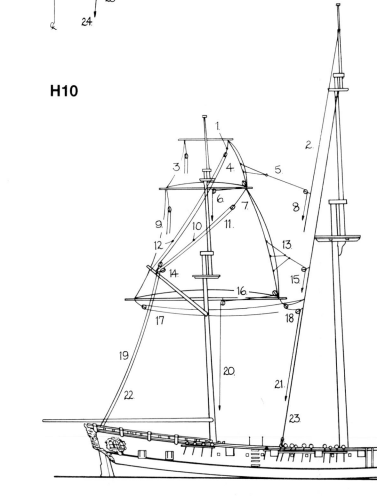

H11

H11 RUNNING RIGGING OF THE MIZZEN GAFF AND BOOM (no scale)

1. Gaff topping lift
2. Gaff jeer tackle
3. Gaff topping lift fall
4. Boom topping lift
5. Boom topping lift fall
6. Jeer tackle fall
7. Boom topping lift tackle
8. Lower block secured to mizzen channel
9. Tackle fall

H12 RUNNING RIGGING OF MIZZEN TOPSAIL AND TOPGALLANT SAILS (fore side of sail to left, after side of sail to right; 1/96 scale)

1. Topgallant yard
2. Buntline pendant block and fall
3. Reef tackle pendant block
4. Jewel block
5. Buntline block
6. Clew line fall block
7. Reef tackle
8. Brace block and pendant
9. Reef tackle fall
10. Standing part of clew line
11. Buntline
12. Clewline fall (running part of clew line)
13. Bowline and bridle
14. Topsail reef tackle pendant block
15. Buntline fall
16. Topsail yard
17. Buntline block seized to tie block
18. Topgallant sheet fall block
19. Jewel block
20. Topsail yard tie block
21. Clewline fall block
22. Reef tackle fall
23. Reef tackle
24. Standing part of clew line
25. Topgallant sheet fall
26. Running part of clewline
27. Clewline fall
28. Buntline
29. Bowline and bridles
30. Topsail sheet
31. Clew block
32. Sheet block
33. Crossjack yard
34. Topsail sheet
35. Crossjack lift block
36. Topsail sheet fall block
37. Fall of the sheet

Mizzen topsail stirrups and footropes are rigged in a similar manner as on the main topsail yard. Mizzen topgallant footropes are rigged in a similar manner to those on the main topgallant yard

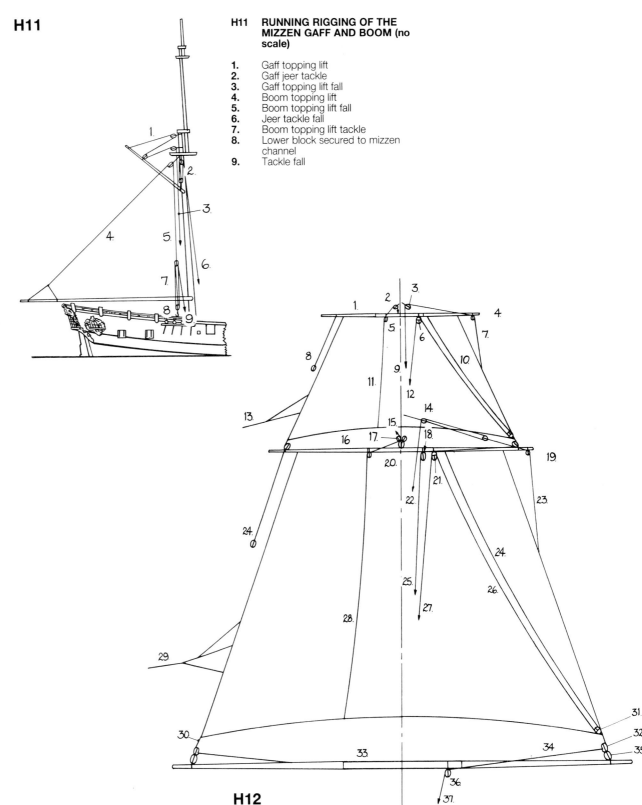

H12

H13 RUNNING RIGGING OF THE MIZZEN GAFFSAIL (no scale)

H13/1 Mizzen gaffsail when set on a boom

H13/2 Mizzen gaffsail when loose footed

1. Peak and throat brails
2. Gaff halyard tackle
3. Peak and throat halyard falls
4. Main gaffsail
5. Loose footed gaffsail
6. Foot brails
7. Foot brail falls
8. Halyard fall
9. Tack tackle and fall
10. Sheave for sheet set in boom
11. Sheet tackle
12. Sheet tackle for loose footed sail
13. Sheet tackle fall

All details of the loose footed gaffsail also apply to the rigging of the main wingsail

H14 RUNNING RIGGING OF THE MAIN WINGSAIL GAFF AND SPRITSAIL (no scale)

H14/1 Side elevation

1. Wingsail gaff topping lift
2. Gaff halyard
3. Single brace block (one fitted to each trestletree)
4. Wingsail gaff yard
5. Topping lift fall
6. Spritsail brace fall (starboard)
7. Spritsail brace fall (port)
8. Jeer halyard fall
9. Running part of spritsail brace
10. Standing part of spritsail brace
11. Spritsail brace block and pendant
12. Spritsail
13. Standing part of spritsail sheet
14. Running part of spritsail sheet
15. Sheet block

H14/2 PLAN VIEW OF SPRITSAIL

1. Footrope
2. Running part of spritsail yard (lift)
3. Spritsail
4. Standing part of spritsail yard lift
5. Lift fall
6. Clew line fall
7. Standing part of clew line
8. Standing lift
9. Clew block

H13/1

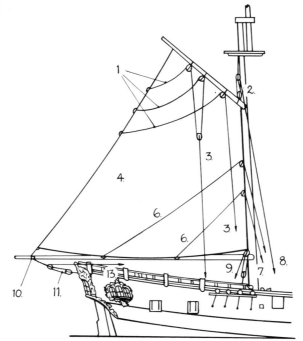

H13/2

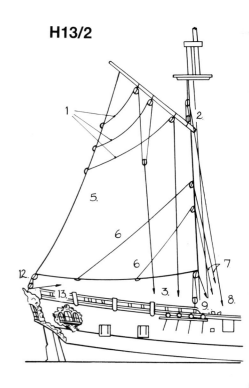

H14/1

H14/2

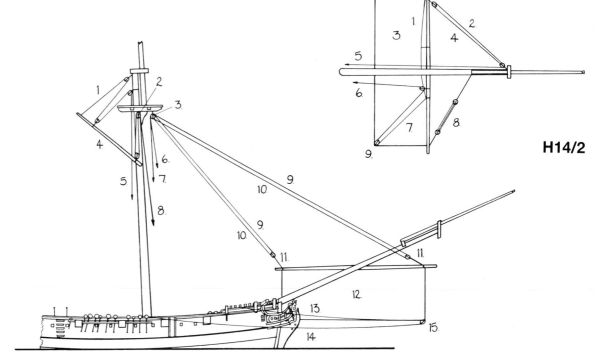

H15/1

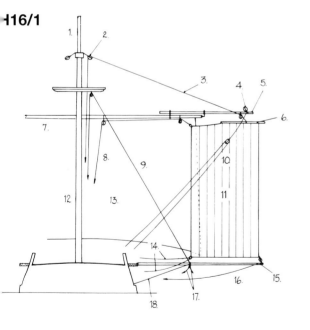

H15/2

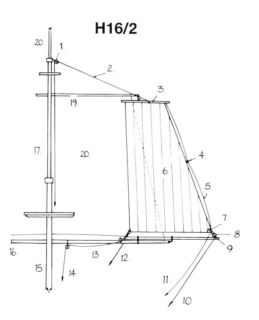

The topsail and topgallant sails were rigged with only two buntlines instead of four. The blocks for these sails were rigged on pendants fastened to their respective mastheads

H16/1

H16/2

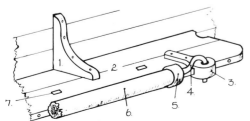

H16/3

109

H Rigging

H17 THE STAYSAILS AND
ASSOCIATED RIGGING (no scale)

H17/1 Elevation

1. Main topgallant stay
2. Standing peak halyard block
3. Main topmast stay
4. Jib staysail stay
5. Peak block
6. Downhauler
7. Main topmast staysail stay
8. Port jib sheets
9. Main topmast staysail
10. Jib
11. Sheet block
12. Downhauler block
13. Tack block, seized to stay
14. Tack fall
15. Staysail stay block (omitted on other sails rigged with a staysail stay for clarity)
16. Staysail stay fall
17. Halyard fall
18. Topmast staysail halyard fall
19. Main preventer stay
20. Main outer staysail stay
21. Main stay
22. Main staysail stay
23. Main outer staysail
24. Sheets (in most cases only one side shown for clarity)
25. Main staysail
26. Mizzen topgallant stay
27. Mizzen topmast staysail stay
28. Mizzen topmast stay
29. Mizzen topmast staysail
30. Mizzen topmast staysail downhauler fall
31. Mizzen stay
32. Mizzen staysail stay
33. Mizzen staysail
34. Combined mizzen topmast staysail stay halyard and downhauler block
35. Mizzen topmast staysail stay fall

Neither the mizzen staysail nor the mizzen topmast staysail were always carried

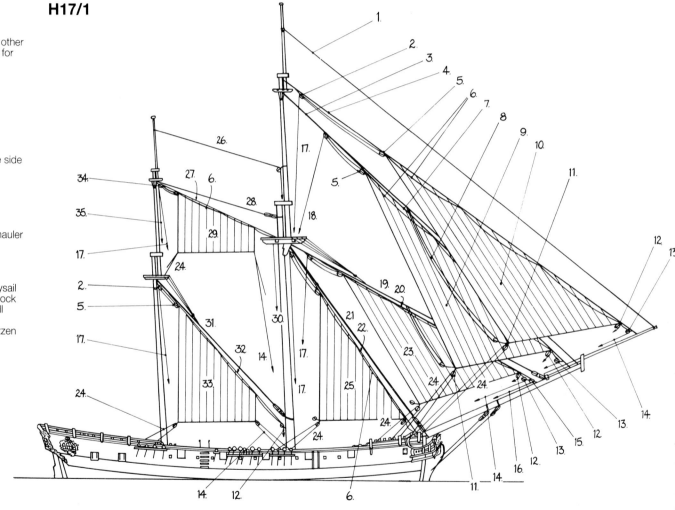

H17/1

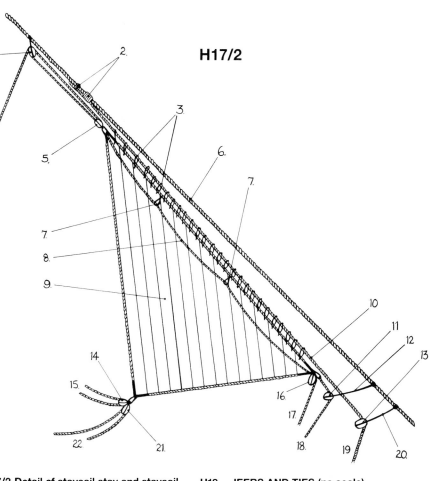

H17/2

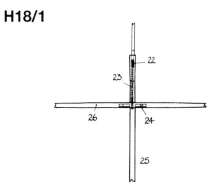

H18/1

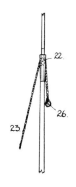

H18/2

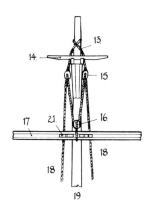

H18/3

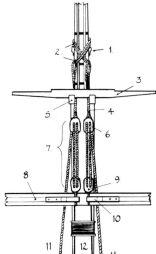
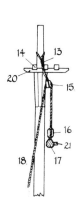
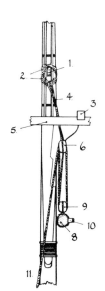

H17/2 Detail of staysail stay and staysail rig

1. Staysail halyard standing block (seized to stay)
2. Seizing of the staysail stay to the topmast stay
3. Robbands (hanks)
4. Staysail halyard fall
5. Staysail halyard peak block
6. Topmast stay (or other relevant stay)
7. Downhauler thimble
8. Downhauler (seized to peak earing)
9. Staysail
10. Staysail stay
11. Staysail tack block
12. Tack block pendant (seized to topmast stay)
13. Staysail stay block (thimble used as an alternative)
14. Port sheet block
15. Port sheets
16. Downhauler block (seized to staysail clew cringle)
17. Downhauler fall
18. Tack fall
19. Staysail stay fall
20. Staysail block pendant (seized to topmast stay)
21. Starboard sheet block
22. Starboard sheets

his applies to all staysails except the jib, hich had its own stay

H18 JEERS AND TIES (no scale)

H18/1 Main topgallant yard

H18/2 Main topsail yard

H18/3 Main yard

1. Masthead cleat
2. Lashing for the jeer strop
3. Crosstrees
4. Jeer strop
5. Trestletree
6. Jeer block (double)
7. Jeer tackle
8. Main yard
9. Lower jeer block (double)
10. Yard sling cleat
11. Fall of the jeers
12. Mainmast
13. Tie pendants
14. Topmast crosstree
15. Standing tie block (single)
16. Single tie block
17. Main topsail yard
18. Falls of the ties
19. Main topmast
20. Topmast trestletree
21. Yard sling cleat
22. Tie sheave set into masthead
23. Tie
24. Yard sling cleat
25. Topgallant mast
26. Main topgallant yard

The yards of the mizzen mast were rigged in a similar manner, except for the mizzen topsail yard, which was rigged as a topgallant yard

111

H19/1

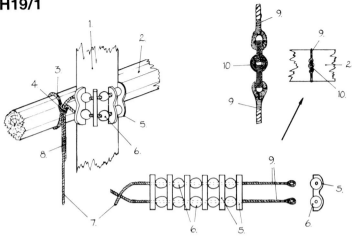

H19/2

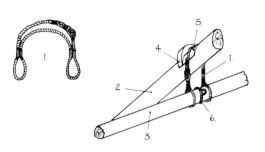

H19   YARD PARRELS AND SLINGS (no scale)

H19/1 General arrangement

1.   Mast
2.   Yard
3.   Sling
4.   Thimble (seized to sling)
5.   Parrel rib
6.   Parrel truck
7.   Fall of the parrel rope
8.   End of the parrel rope seized to fall
9.   Eyes of the parrel rope (to pass around yard)
10.   Rose lashing

H19/2 Spritsail yard

1.   Sling
2.   Bowsprit
3.   Spritsail yard
4.   Saddle
5.   Leather pad (apron)
6.   Halyard sling

H20   DETAIL OF THE GAFF, WINGSAIL GAFF AND BOOM PARRELS (no scale)

H20/1 Gaff yard (this drawing also applies to the wingsail gaff)

1.   Gaff
2.   Gaff halyard tackle
3.   Mizzen mast (or mainmast)
4.   Iron hoop
5.   Halyard tackle block and hook
6.   Eyebolt (for above)
7.   Jaws
8.   Monkey fist end of parrel rope passing through jaws
9.   Parrel truck
10.   Parrel rope

H20/2 Boom (This drawing applies to mizzen mast only, if fitted)

1.   Boom
2.   Iron hoops
3.   Mizzen mast
4.   Parrel truck
5.   Parrel rope
6.   Jaws
7.   Mast saddle
8.   Monkey fist end of parrel rope passing through jaws
9.   Mast saddle support brackets

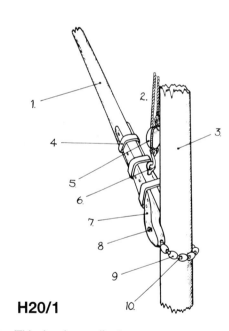

H20/1

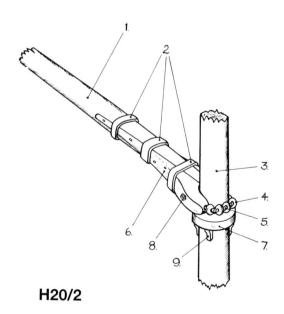

H20/2

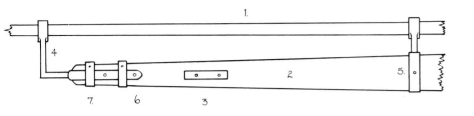

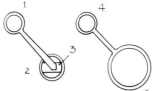

H21/1

H21/2

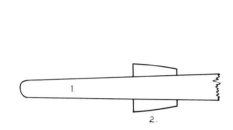

H21/3

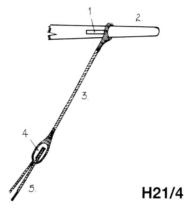

H21/4

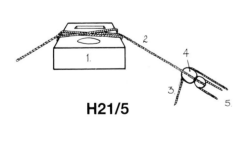

H21/5

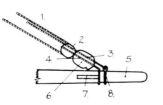

H21/6

H21 YARDARM FITTINGS AND RIGGING

H21/1 Stunsail boom and yardarm (1/24 scale)

1. Upper stunsail boom
2. Lower yard
3. Yardarm cleat
4. Outer stunsail boom iron
5. Inner stunsail boom iron
6. Boom iron yoke
7. Retaining hoops

H21/2 Boom iron hoops (1/48 scale)

1. Outer stunsail boom iron hoop
2. Hoop around yardarm
3. Boom iron yoke
4. Inner stunsail boom iron hoop
5. Hoop around yard

H21/3 Plan view of yardarm (1/48 scale)

1. Yardarm
2. Yardarm cleat

H21/4 Yardarm and brace pendant (no scale)

1. Yardarm cleat
2. Yardarm
3. Brace pendant
4. Brace block
5. Running part of the brace

H21/5 Lower mast cap (no scale)

1. Lower mast cap
2. Long tackle pendant
3. Fall of the lift
4. Long tackle block
5. Running part of the lift

H21/6 Yardarm and associated blocks (no scale)

1. Running part of the lift
2. Single block seized to topsail sheet block
3. Standing part of the lift
4. Lift and sheet block strop
5. Yardarm
6. Topsail sheet block
7. Yardarm cleat
8. Strop for standing part of lift

113

H Rigging

H22 ARRANGEMENT OF YARD BLOCKS (no scale)

H22/1 Topgallant yard

H22/2 Topsail yard

H22/3 Main yard

1. Main yard
2. Jeer blocks
3. Sling cleat
4. Quarter block for horses (foot ropes)
5. Lower stunsail inner halyard block
6. Buntline block
7. Clewline block
8. Buntline block
9. Block for the tricing line
10. Inner stunsail boom iron
11. Horse block
12. Lower stunsail inner halyard block
13. Main yard lift block
14. Main topsail sheet block
15. Outer stunsail boom iron
16. Main brace block
17. Yard tackle
18. Topsail yard
19. Tie block
20. Sling cleat
21. Clewline block
22. Buntline block
23. Topsail yard lift block
24. Brace block
25. Stunsail yard boom iron
26. Jewel block for the topmast stunsail halyard
27. Topgallant yard
28. Tie block
29. Sling cleats
30. Clewline block
31. Brace block and pendant
32. Topgallant yard lift block
33. Jewel block for topgallant stunsail yard halyard (if fitted)

All blocks associated with the studding sails are fitted on the yards of the main mast only, the remaining blocks correspond to the yards of both the mainmast and the mizzen mast. Blocks for the foot ropes were not always fitted on the mizzen crossjack yard

H23 METHOD OF SCARPHING THE YARDS (no scale)

1. Side elevation showing scarph face of one half of the yard
2. Plan of one half of the yard
3. Plan of opposite half of the yard
4. Dowel (or coak) holes, joining the two portions

H22/1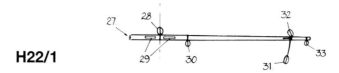

H22/2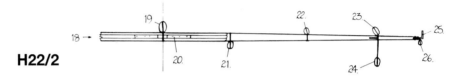

H22/3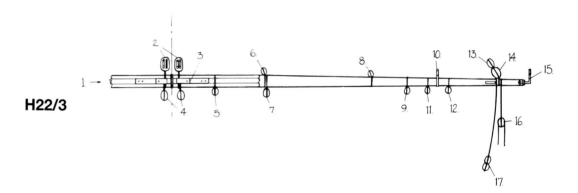

H23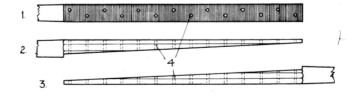

H24   MAST HEADS (no scale)

H24/1 Detail of main lower mast head top

1. Main topmast shrouds
2. Mainmast cap
3. Main yard lift block strop (pendant)
4. Hole for main topmast
5. Ratlines
6. Mizzen topmast stay
7. Main yard lift long tackle block
8. Eye for top ropes
9. Strops for jeer pendants
10. Main yard lifts
11. Topmast shroud stave
12. Mizzen topmast stay deadeye
13. Topmast shroud lashing and deadeye
14. Main yard lift fall
15. Main top rail
16. Mizzen topmast staysail stay (if carried)
17. Mizzen topmast staysail block (if fitted)
18. Topmast shroud lower deadeye
19. Deadeye plate
20. Deadeye lanyards
21. Bolster

22. Lower mast shroud eyes—starboard side indicated in detail, port side left blank
23. Toggles securing buntline blocks
24. Main top gunwale
25. Jeer strop
26. Batten
27. Iron plate for topmast heel fid
28. Crowsfeet
29. Topmast deadeye and futtock shroud plates
30. Spritsail brace and main course buntline block
31. Studding sail boom topping lift and inner buntline fall block
32. Standing jeer block
33. Bibs
34. Futtock shroud hook
35. Studding sail boom topping lift fall
36. Spritsail brace and outer buntline fall block
37. Futtock shroud
38. Outer buntline

39. Outer buntline fall
40. Spritsail brace fall
41. Inner buntline fall
42. Burton pendant
43. Mast woolding and bands
44. Spritsail brace
45. Stay mouse and eye
46. Running jeer block
47. Studding sail boom topping
48. Main backstay
49. Futtock shroud stave
50. Main yard parrels
51. Inner buntline block
52. Main yard
53. Main shrouds
54. Main course inner buntline
55. Seizing and standing part of clewline
56. Footrope seizing
57. Clewline fall
58. Foremost main shroud (swifter)
59. Main topsail sheet block and sheet fall
60. Main jeer fall pendant
61. Mainmast

62. Main yard sling cleats
63. Foot ropes
64. Main topsail sheet fall
65. Main topsail sheet block
66. Clewline fall
67. Main stay (note worming)
68. Running part of clewline
69. Main preventer stay
70. Topsail sheet

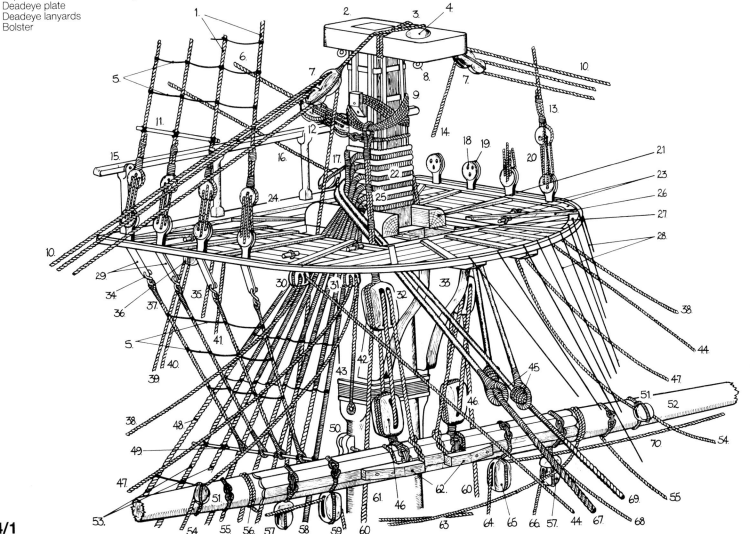

H24/1

115

H Rigging

H24/2 Detail of the main topmast head

1. Main topgallant shrouds
2. Main topmast cap
3. Hole for main topgallant mast
4. Ratlines
5. Block for topmast stunsail yard halyard
6. Topmast head
7. Single tie block and standing tie rope pendant strope
8. Crosstrees
9. Single tie block pendant
10. Standing part of tie
11. Eyes of the topmast shrouds and backstays
12. Bolster
13. Standing buntline block
14. Trestletrees
15. Single tie block
16. Futtock shrouds
17. Topmast stay mouse and eye
18. Sister block (seized to shrouds)
19. Buntline fall
20. Buntline block
21. Topsail yard lift (leading to top part of sister block)
22. Topmast shrouds and ratlines
23. Double tie block
24. Parrel rope seizing
25. Reef tackle fall
26. Running part of reef tackle (leading to bottom part of sister block)
27. Main topmast running backstay
28. Main topmast backstay
29. Buntline
30. Yard battens
31. Topgallant sheet
32. Running part of clewline
33. Topsail standing clewline block
34. Clewline fall
35. Topgallant sheet quarter block
36. Tie fall
37. Topgallant sheet fall
38. Topsail lift fall
39. Buntline fall
40. Main topmast
41. Footrope (horse)
42. Yard sling cleats
43. Standing part of topsail clewline
44. Topsail running clewline block
45. Main topmast stay
46. Main topsail yard
47. Buntline (fall to topsail clew)
48. Footrope seizing
49. Buntline block

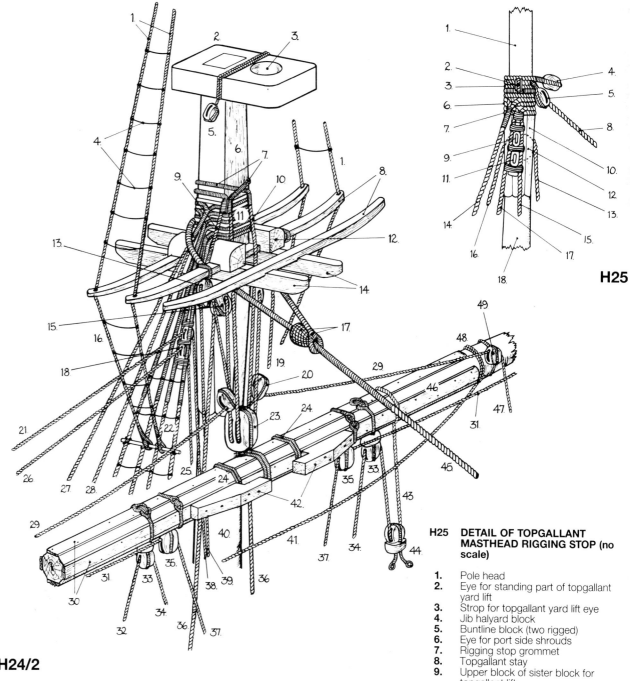

H24/2

H25

H25   DETAIL OF TOPGALLANT MASTHEAD RIGGING STOP (no scale)

1. Pole head
2. Eye for standing part of topgallant yard lift
3. Strop for topgallant yard lift eye
4. Jib halyard block
5. Buntline block (two rigged)
6. Eye for port side shrouds
7. Rigging stop grommet
8. Topgallant stay
9. Upper block of sister block for topgallant lift
10. Hounds and rigging stop
11. Lower block of sister block for topgallant reef tackle fall
12. Sheave in mast for topgallant yard tie
13. Topgallant yard tie
14. Standing topgallant backstay
15. First topgallant shroud
16. Tie fall
17. Second topgallant shroud
18. Lower part of topgallant mast

126 FITTINGS ASSOCIATED WITH THE RIGGING (no scale)

1. Mizzen mast
2. Belaying pins
3. Pin rack attached to mast
4. Timberhead of kevel block
5. Sheave
6. Kevel cleat
7. Sheave
8. Sheave block
9. Sheave for mizzen course brace
10. Cleat for mizzen course brace
11. Pin rail (for gaff vangs, peak halyards and gaff sail sheet)
12. Sheave block for main brace
13. Kevel block (gaff halyard to port, gaff topping lift to starboard)
14. Kevel cleats (for main sheet)
15. Timber cleat used for second running backstay (if required)
16. Timber cleat for main staysail sheet
17. Kevel cleat timberhead
18. Main jeer bitts
19. Main topsail and sheet bitts
20. Cleat for spritsail sheet
21. Cleat for main course tack
22. Timberheads
23. Mizzen channel and deadeyes
24. Pin rail (fitted to mizzen shrouds)
25. Quarterdeck breast rail
26. Mizzen mast
27. Main topgallant backstay stool and deadeye
28. Main channels and deadeyes
29. Mainmast
30. Forecastle breast rail

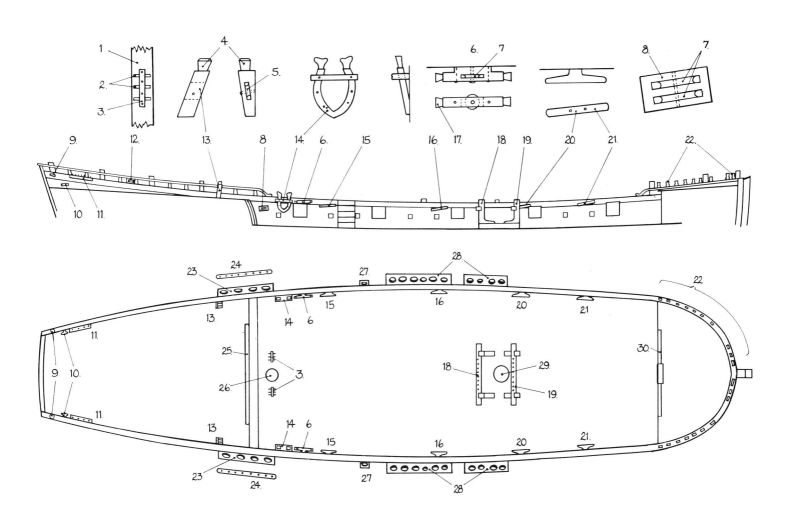

H26

H27   VARIETIES OF BLOCK (1/24 scale)

1. Common single-sheaved block, side elevation
2. Common single-sheaved block, end elevation
3. Double-sheaved block (type used for jeers)
4. Treble-sheaved block (type used for catblock)
5. Sister block
6. Long tackle block
7. Sheet block
8. Spritsail sheet block
9. Shoulder block (type used for clewlines)
10. Deadeye with concave groove for shrouds
11. Deadeye with flat groove for chain plates
12. Shoe block (used for buntline falls)
13. Lignum vitae sheave
14. Sheave pin
15. Score for pendant rope

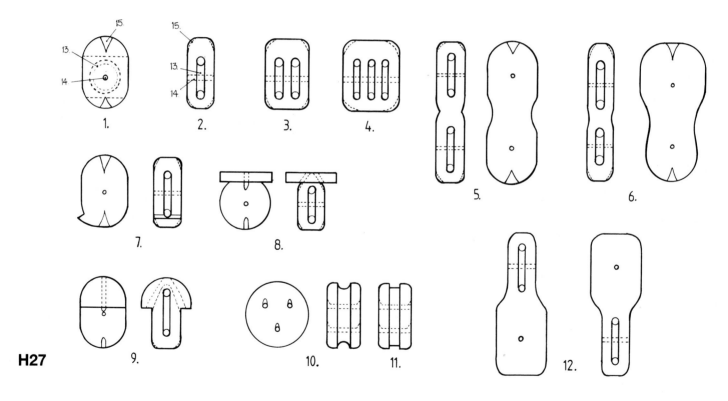

H27

Sails

1/1

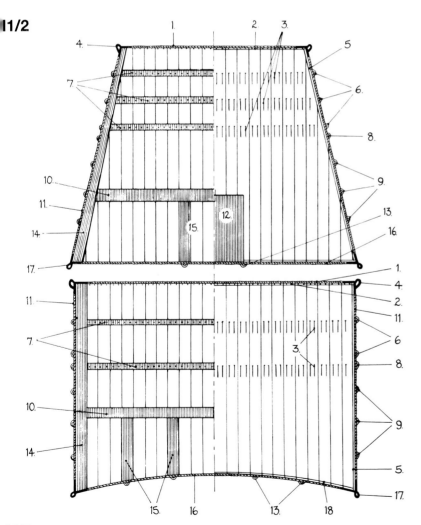

I1/2

I1/3

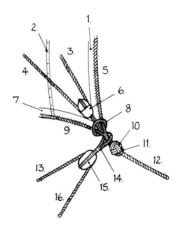

I1/3

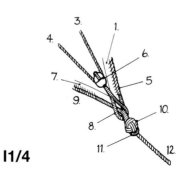

I1/4

1. Head bolt rope
2. Head seam and roband gaskets
3. Reef points
4. Earing
5. Leech seam
6. Reef cringles
7. Reef linings
8. Leechline cringle
9. Bowline and bridle cringle
10. Middle beam lining
11. Leech bolt rope
12. Top lining
13. Buntline cringle
14. Leech lining
15. Buntline lining
16. Foot bolt rope
17. Clew
18. Foot seam

The fore side of the sail is shown on the left, the after side to the right

1. Leech seam
2. Tabling of sail cloths
3. Standing part of clewline
4. Running part of clewline
5. Leech bolt rope
6. Clew block
7. Foot seam
8. Clew block strop
9. Foot bolt rope
10. Monkey fist end of tack
11. Clew
12. Tack
13. Running part of sheet
14. Sheet block strop
15. Sheet block
16. Standing part of sheet

Mizzen square sail clews and tacks are identical, and the main course clew and tack is identical to that of the main topsail

119

I Sails

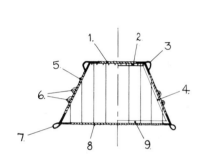

I2/1

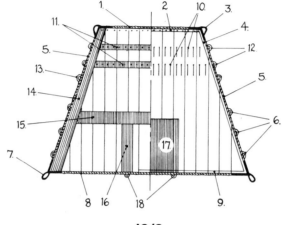

I2/2

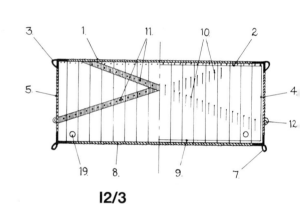

I2/3

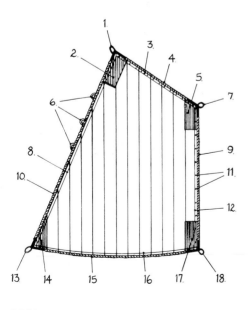

I3/1

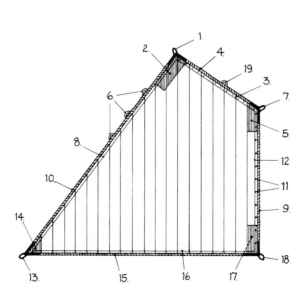

I3/2

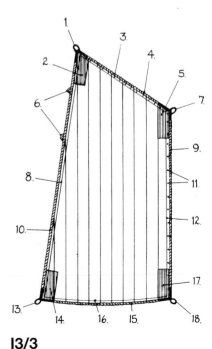

I3/3

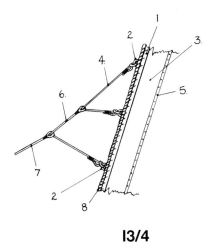

I3/4

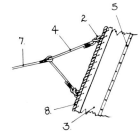

I3/5

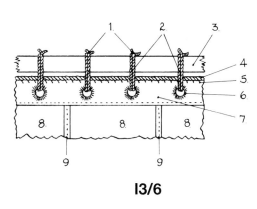

I3/6

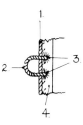

I3/7

I3/4   **Topsail and course bridles (no scale)**

I3/5   **Topgallant bridles (no scale)**

1. Leech seam
2. Bridle cringle
3. Sail cloth
4. Bridle
5. Cloth tabling
6. Second bridle
7. Bowline
8. Bolt rope

I3/6   **Detail of robands and gaskets (no scale)**

1. Reef knots
2. Robands
3. Yard
4. Head bolt rope
5. Stitch of sail to bolt rope
6. Roband gasket
7. Head seam
8. Sail cloths
9. Cloth tabling

I3/7   **Detail of cringle (no scale)**

1. Bolt rope
2. Cringle
3. Cringle gaskets
4. Leech seam

I Sails

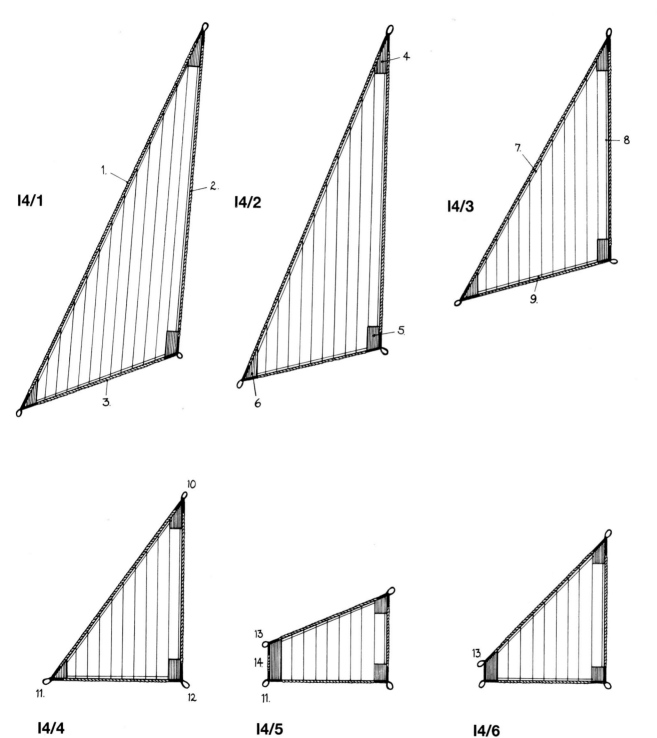

I4/1

I4/2

I4/3

I4/4

I4/5

I4/6

I4 STAYSAILS (1/192 scale)

Port side shown to reveal lining details

I4/1 Jib

I4/2 Main topmast staysail

I4/3 Outer staysail

I4/4 Main staysail

I4/5 Mizzen topmast staysail (not always carried)

I4/6 Mizzen staysail (not always carried)

1. Luff bolt rope
2. Leach bolt rope
3. Foot bolt rope
4. Peak lining
5. Clew lining
6. Tack lining
7. Luff seam
8. Leach seam
9. Foot seam
10. Peak cringle
11. Tack cringle
12. Clew cringle (sheet cringle)
13. Luff cringle
14. Bunt

5 MAIN LOWER AND TOPSAIL STUDDING SAILS (STUNSAILS)
(1/192 scale)

I5/1 **Main topmast stunsail**

I5/2 **Main lower stunsail**

1. Peak linings
2. Head bolt rope
3. Earings
4. Reef lining
5. Reef cringle
6. Leach bolt rope
7. After side of main topmast stunsail
8. Luff bolt rope
9. Seams
10. Fore side of main topmast stunsail
11. Clew lining
12. Foot bolt rope
13. Clew cringles
14. Halyard cringle
15. After side of main lower stunsail
16. Fore side of main lower stunsail

Sail sizes have been estimated from references to sail sizes for two-masted sloops and ketches, PRO-Adm 96/17. It is not clear whether the *Granado* was furnished with studding sails when employed as a bomb ship, but it is very likely that they would have been carried when she served as a sloop. Note that only the port side sails are shown

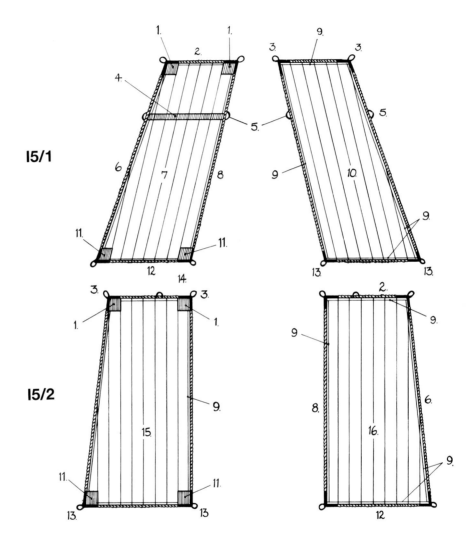

J The ship's boats

As noted above, the exact size and type of boats carried of the *Granado* is uncertain; the evidence suggests that her complement of boats followed that of sloops and similar sized naval vessels of the period: one 24ft pinnace and/or a 16ft long boat. Unfortunately, suitable drawings and source material for these two types of boat is scarce, so reconstructed plans from the available sources are given here.

J1   **RECONSTRUCTION OF A 24FT PINNACE (1/48 scale)**

J1/1   **Body plan**

J1/2   **Sheer and profile**

J1/3   **Half breadth plan**

J1/4   **Detailed plan**

1.	Rudder
2.	Transom
3.	Sternsheet transom
4.	After locker
5.	Sternsheets
6.	Sternsheet bottom boards
7.	Gunwale
8.	Thwart
9.	Sheer strake
10.	Stringer supporting the thwarts
11.	Rowlock
12.	Fore thwart
13.	Peak locker
14.	Stem post
15.	Rabbet
16.	Keel (showing rabbet)
17.	Stern post
18.	Second waterline
19.	First waterline
20.	Transverse sternsheet thwart
21.	Thwart pillar
22.	Thwart knee (inverse)
23.	Hole and housing for mast
24.	Peak
25.	Apron (false stern)

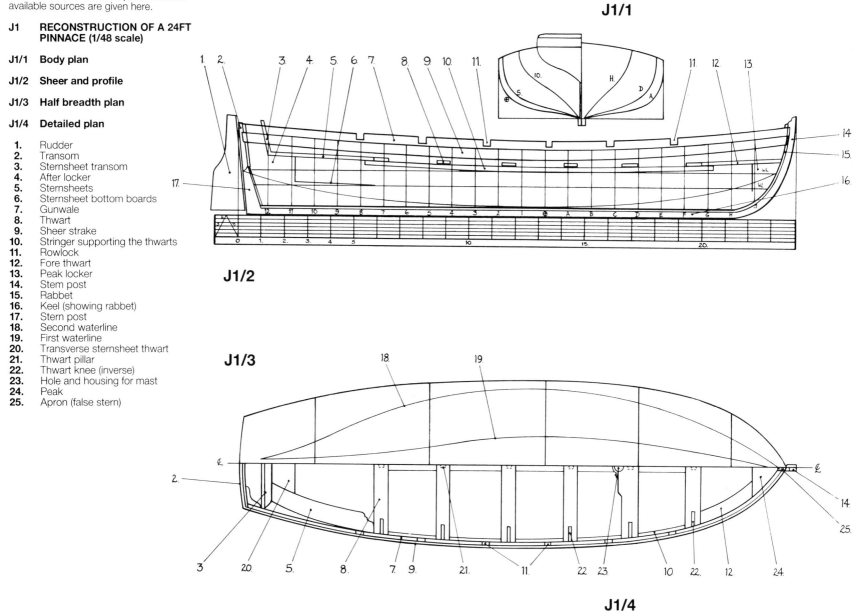

J1/1

J1/2

J1/3

J1/4

**J2 RECONSTRUCTION OF A 16FT
LONG BOAT (1/48 scale)**

J2/1 Body plan

J2/2 Sheer and profile

J2/3 Half breadth plan

J2/4 Detailed plan

1. Sternsheet transom
2. Sternsheets
3. Sternsheet bottom boards
4. Thwarts
5. Rowlock
6. Gunwale
7. Sheer strake
8. Stringer supporting the thwarts
9. Apron (false post)
10. Stem post
11. Rabbet
12. Keel (showing rabbet)
13. Rudder
14. Transom
15. Stern post
16. Second waterline
17. First waterline
18. Transverse sternsheet thwart
19. Keelson
20. Thwart knee (inverse)

J2/1

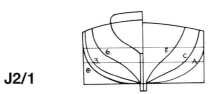

J2/2

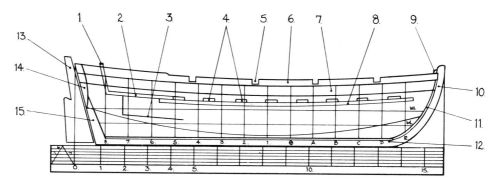

J2/3

J2/4

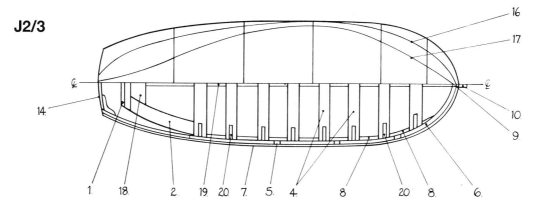